INSIGHT: DETERMINANTS OF SMES INTERNATIONALISATION IN INDONESIA

By

RITA R. PIDANI PHD

FRANK W. AGBOLA PHD

AMIR MAHMOOD PHD

Title : Insight: Determinants of SMEs Internationalisation in Indonesia
Authors: Dr. Rita R. Pidani, Dr. Frank W. Agbola, Dr. Amir Mahmood
Cover Design: Mohsen Rahmandoust
Publisher: Supreme Century, USA
ISBN: 978-1939123824

ABSTRACT

This paper investigates managerial and organisational factors affecting export development of manufacturing small and medium-sized enterprises (SMEs) in Indonesia. Export development of SMEs has been widely researched. However, little is known of how and why exports as part of internationalisation process take place in developing countries and this lack of evidence in the literature provides a strong rationale for this study. A review of the literature suggests that an investigation of export development should include the broad range of managerial and organisational factors as the key driving forces influencing the process. This line of reasoning highlights the role played by firm-specific resources and management characteristics in shaping the export development process.

To meet its research objectives, a quantitative method was employed. A personally administered survey was conducted in 2015, involving 197 owners and/or managers of manufacturing SMEs using a structured questionnaire. The data was analysed using the statistical package SPSS. AMOS was employed to test the underlying model and address various hypotheses. The results are largely deductive and are presented in quantitative-themes.

The findings suggest the following: Firstly, export development of manufacturing SMEs in Indonesia is constrained by a lack of knowledge to identify foreign business opportunities, lack of resources to develop new products, difficulty in maintaining control over foreign middlemen, and verbal and non-verbal language differences. These are areas where export strategies could be addressed and improved. Secondly, the results indicate that interrelated factors influence export development of Indonesian manufacturing SMEs. Firm size, firm age, firm location, managerial age and language proficiency were particularly significant in determining the level of export development undertaken. Thirdly, the study also found that the key driver of export development of manufacturing SMEs in Indonesia is profit and opportunities in overseas markets. This study provides strong empirical evidence to suggest that to improve export performance there is the need to enhance economic and social development in Indonesia. This could be achieved through a more transparent government policy, promoting coherence among agencies supporting SMEs export development and adopting structured and relevant export development strategies in Indonesia.

TABLE OF CONTENTS

Contents

LIST OF FIGURES

LIST OF TABLES

LIST OF ABBREVIATIONS

AGFI	Average Goodness of Fit Index
AMOS	Analysis of a Moment Structures
APEC	Asia-Pacific Economic Cooperation
BAPPENAS	*Badan Perencanaan dan Pembangunan Nasional* (National Planning and Development Board)
CFI	Comparative Fit Index
GFI	Goodness of Fit Index
KEMENPERIN	Indonesian Ministry of Industry
LEs	Large Enterprises
MOCSME	Ministry of Cooperatives and Small and Medium-sized Enterprises.
DGNED	Directorate General for National Export Development
NFI	Normed Fit Index
OECD	Organisation for Economic Cooperation and Development
RMSEA	Root Mean Square Error of Approximation
SEM	Structural Equation Modeling
SMEs	Small and Medium-sized Enterprises
SRMR	Squared Multiple Correlations
TLI	Tucker Lewis Index
WTO	World Trade Organisation

CHAPTER ONE

INTRODUCTION

1.1 Background of the Study

In today's global economy, Small and Medium Enterprises (abbreviated herein, henceforth SMEs) are increasingly becoming important as a significant source of employment and wealth creation in both developed and developing countries. The SMEs are capable of stimulating job creation, of developing crucial capability of innovations in both product and services, and of promoting diversification within an economy. An economy that meets the needs of its entrepreneurs in SMEs increases its chances of job growth which then translates into a vibrant economy. In particular, in developing countries where large government enterprises are downsizing in response to the changing global economy (WTO's website, 2016), the creation of a healthy business environment will help support small and medium businesses and this in turn will help with the retention of skilled workers. It is therefore pertinent to understand the operation of SMEs and establish effective support systems to help boost growth within these enterprises. In this study, SMEs are defined as firms having less than 300 workers.

It is widely acknowledged in the international trade literature that exports have become increasingly important for a firm's survival in today's global environment (Bartlett and Ghoshal, 2000; Katsikeas, 2003; Leonidou et al., 2002). Exporting, as the most direct and common way for manufacturers to do business in foreign markets, is still considered an attractive and less risky method particularly for SMEs as it does not require as much resource commitment as other modes of international entry such as *licensing, strategic alliances, joint ventures, or international subsidiaries* (Hutchinson et al., 2006, Rasheed, 2005). Through this outward-oriented strategy, firms in developing countries, such as Indonesia, are linked to the international system of trade and payments. Accordingly, trade becomes the engine of economic growth among countries as well as for firms operating within them (Wignaraja et al., 1991). The premise of opening up economies to reap various benefits of international trade has also impelled the Indonesian government to reverse much of the imbalance created by past inward-oriented development policies. In recent years, this outward oriented strategy has emerged as the dominant strategy outperforming import substitution industrialisation which was once the orthodox thrust of development economics in the country (Soesastro and Basri, 2005). Despite the continuing debate on the negative aspects of this strategy in the context of economic breakdown in Latin America and the Carribean economies (Hadad et al., 2010), the more positive effects taking place in countries such as Japan, Korea, and more recently China (where exporting has led onto foreign direct investment abroad and hence the development of internationalisation), have put forth the importance of promoting manufactured exports in Indonesia.

There is growing recognition among policy makers in both developed and developing countries that this export outward-oriented strategy can solve the trade deficit problems faced by many countries (see for example Dollar, 1992; Edwards, 1998; Sachs and Warner, 1995). This has generated a plethora of studies that examine firm-level organisational and managerial characteristics and how these impact on exports. In the international trade literature, a number of studies have examined problems perceived by firms at various stages of export development. For a review, see for example, Bilkey, 1978; Ahmed et al. 2004; Katsikeas and Piercy, 1991, Suarez-ortega, 2003. These studies conclude that by identifying problems faced by exporting firms, corporate and public policy makers who deal with export promotion programs will have a better perspective in formulating and implementing more effective trade policies and national export promotion programs (Gray, 1997; Suarez-ortega, 2003; Wilkinson and Brouthers, 2006).

Despite the growing evidence of the importance of exports in sustaining growth of an economy, a review of the literature revealed a concentration of studies that focused on export barriers of SMEs in developed and/or newly industrialised countries (Leonidou, 2004; Tesform and Lutz, 2006), with very limited research on developing country SMEs. Given the differences that exist in developed and developing countries, it is inappropriate to generalise the findings of previous studies to developing countries, and in particular, to the Indonesian context. Although the level of industrialisation and economic development in these developing countries might not be as advanced as those of developed nations, Dominiguez and Sequeira in Aulakh and Kotabe (2000) argued that developing countries can also gain from trade liberalisation which potentially will enhance their competitiveness by providing opportunities to develop distinctive products, resources, and strategies. Clearly, it is important to investigate the barriers faced by developing country-based firms in order to validate the general application of these previous findings to such nations.

Like many developing countries, Indonesia is heavily dependent on the rest of the world. The Indonesian economy with its longstanding tradition in international trade has experienced severe stress in the last two decades and has undergone major macroeconomic and trade policy reforms. These changes are likely to have impacted on the way SMEs conduct their activities in Indonesia. Most of the SMEs have for a long-time been recognised as a large provider of employment and a potential source of export revenue. They constitute more than 90 per cent of all firms outside the agricultural sector (Indonesian Ministry of Cooperatives and SMEs abbreviated herein, henceforth MOCSME's website, 2009).

The SMEs in Indonesia contribute immensely to growth in the production, distribution, and service sectors of the economy. According to Indonesian MOCSME's, in 2016, of all formal and informal enterprises, there was an estimated 787,598 SMEs operating across all industries and sectors and employing

8.9 million of the 112.8 million people employed by Micro, Small and Medium Enterprises (abbreviated herein, henceforth MSMEs) (*MOCSMEs, 2016*). The contribution of SME's to the country's GDP increased slightly from 2.1 billion in 2007 to 2.7 billion rupiah in 2016. This represented 23.2 per cent of total GDP in 2016, suggesting that SMEs are contributing a smaller share of GDP than that of the large enterprises (abbreviated herein, henceforth LEs) (*MOCSMEs*, 2016). The Micro Enterprises (abbreviated herein, henceforth MIEs) are the biggest contributor to the country's GDP in 2016, accounting for 42.7 per cent of total GDP. Despite this, the worth of investment by SMEs across all industries and sectors grew from 44.6 per cent of total worth of investment in 2007 to 50.5 per cent in 2016, while that of large enterprises fell marginally from 47.5 per cent to 42.1 per cent in the respective period. These juxtaposing facts, as well as SMEs palpable role as downstream assembling industry, have forced the Indonesian government to change their policy strategies by focusing on promoting SMEs as a vehicle for achieving economic growth and development within the country.

As part of this reform, the Indonesian government has introduced successive trade policy reforms to minimize the strong anti-export bias of the past protectionist policies. The primary goal of these trade policy reforms has been to convert the import-substituting pattern of industrialisation during the oil boom era of the late 1970s and early 1980's to an export-promoting one (Wie, 2006). It is expected that this shift, from reliance on the oil and gas sectors to other sectors of the economy, particularly the manufacturing sector, would create confidence among entrepreneurs and investors thereby stimulating non-oil exports to offset the decline in tax revenue derived from oil exports.

Prior to 2000, the major focus of the Indonesian government's policies was large enterprises within the manufacturing sector. The role and contribution of SMEs was initially regarded as trivial in the Indonesian government's agenda due to the inherent limitations of size and resources of SMEs. Following the Asian crisis which saw LEs hit hard and SMEs rebounding from the shocks (Berry et al. 2002; Asia Foundation's website 2009; Wengel and Rodriguez, 2006), there was growing recognition among policy makers in Indonesia that SMEs are capable of ensuring continued growth of the economy. With the SMEs turning out to be more resilient than the highly indebted conglomerates, and exhibiting their flexibility and agility to the ever-changing market conditions, SMEs through their exports, are seen as capable of playing a key role in improving the balance of payments of the Indonesian economy (Urata, 2000). In a study conducted by the Asian Development Bank (ADB), the contribution of SMEs to total non-oil and gas exports after the Asian economic crisis of 1997 increased by 11 per cent (ADB, 2004). The recent data from the MOCSMEs showed that the figure stood at 14.4 per cent in 2017 (MOCSMES, 2018). Thus, the SMEs and MIEs contribution were relatively minor and tended to decline over the time.

Clearly, SMEs in Indonesia still face a number of challenges which tend to constrain their potential to grow. This study, therefore, aims to enhance an understanding of the export behaviour of SMEs by investigating export barriers facing SMEs and to explore the efficacy of the Indonesian government's SMEs export promotion strategies.

1.2 Problem Statement

The need to strengthen the exports of the manufacturing sector in particular implies that more outward-oriented approach is needed to help assist Indonesia to achieve significant economic growth and development. The efforts of the Indonesian government to stimulate economic development through import substitution of locally produced goods needs to be combined with an export expansion approach to optimize gains obtained from trade. World trade has grown dramatically over the years, climbing from approximately forty billion US dollars in 1945 to nearly twelve trillion in the year 2017 (WTO' website, 2017), so Indonesia needs to strategically position itself in the changing global trade environment. To achieve this requires a greater understanding of the structure, conduct and performance of SMEs in Indonesia and a further identification of the barriers hindering their export development.

The Indonesian economy has experienced trade deficit pressure throughout the period of 1985 to 1996 (*Bappenas'* website, 2016; Erwidodo, 1999). This pressure, coupled with domestic economic problems such as low foreign investment levels, bureaucratic red tape and high unemployment, has forced the Indonesian government to embark on a policy of stimulating growth in the export sector. To this end, the Indonesian government implemented a deregulatory policy reform aimed at simplifying the requirements and procedures for exports, and the development of an export-import infrastructure to help promote and sustain export growth in the manufacturing SME sector in Indonesia (*Bappenas'* website, 2018).

The benefits derived from international trade, and exporting in particular, have also become important grounds for SMEs to increasingly get involved in international operations. In the past, the Indonesian government has overlooked the capability of SMEs and has paid too much attention to LEs, with a number of policies directly in favour of developing them. For SMEs, most of the policies have been inward-looking. SMEs were regarded as infant industries and provided with some privileges which protected them from global competition. However, the experience of the 1990s Asian financial crisis suggests that SMEs could benefit from the export-oriented strategy accorded to the LEs. This notion is based on the premise that policy-makers, with their export stimulation and assistance schemes, have a good understanding of the operations of SMEs.

Recent evidence also suggests an evolving need for understanding further the determinants and constraints facing SMEs' exports. One motivation behind this study is the responsiveness of SMEs to the changing global environment. In periods of declining exports, SMEs may respond in a variety of ways. For instance, they may engage in intensification in the production of products for export or expand the production base through diversification. Given the changing global economy in recent times, and the limited research on the operations of SMEs in Indonesia, it is pertinent that we investigate the perceptions of exporting and non-exporting SMEs with regards to the constraints facing them. In addition, we identify the factors influencing export involvement of SMEs in Indonesia. This would aid in policy formulation and implementation to assist their export drive and thus foster sustained economic growth and development in the Indonesian economy.

1.3 Objectives and Hypotheses of the Study

1.3.1 Objectives

The main objective of this study is to undertake an empirical investigation of the particular organizational and managerial determinants of the different aspects of a firm's export development process of manufacturing SMEs in Indonesia.

1.3.2 Hypotheses

Based on the extant literature and the objectives of this study, the following hypotheses have been developed:

H1: Manager's age has a negative effect on the level of export development, thus it has a negative effect on export propensity and intensity.

H2: Manager's educational has a positive effect on the level of export development, thus it has a positive effect on export propensity and intensity.

H3: Manager's experience has a positive effect on the level of export development, thus it has a positive effect on export propensity and intensity.

H4: Manager's foreign language proficiency has a positive effect on the level of export development, thus it has a positive effect on export propensity and intensity.

H5: Firm's size has a positive effect on export development and export propensity, but a negative effect on export intensity.

H6: Firm's age has a negative effect on the level of export development, thus it has a negative effect on export propensity and intensity.

H7: Firm's geographic market development has a positive effect on the level of export development, thus it has a positive effect on export propensity and intensity.

H8: Firm's location has a negative effect on the level of export development, thus it has a negative effect on export propensity and intensity.

1.4 Methodology of the Research

Based on the objectives of this study, a questionnaire was administered to elicit information on the organisational and managerial characteristics of SMEs in the manufacturing sector in Indonesia. The questionnaire contains a series of questions which were compiled following the review of previous empirical studies on export involvement. The structured questionnaire was pre-tested for clarity, difficulty and ease of response before the execution of the full-scale study. The pilot survey was administered to 24 SMEs from each of the 4 major provinces with manufacturing SMEs. The questionnaire was revised following the pilot survey and subsequently personally administered to achieve higher respondent participation. In the end, 200 surveys of SME operators were usable, which is considered satisfactory for subsequent analyses (Comrey, 1978; Gorsuch, 1983; Guilford, 1954; Hair et al. 1998; Lindeman et al. 1980; Long, 1983).

The study focuses on manufacturing SMEs in Indonesia engaged in the garment, footwear, and furniture and wood products industries. The selection is based on their significant role and contribution to the Indonesian economy (for further discussion, see Section 2.6 of Chapter 2). The analysis is narrowed to only manufactured goods due to their major role in the industrialisation of the Indonesian economy in the last two decades and the increasing share of Indonesia's manufacturing SMEs in recent years.

Following the data collection, the sample was grouped into four levels of export development. This follows the approach used by Leonidou and Katsikeas (1996), Suarez-Ortega (2003), and Jansson and Sandberg (2008), whereby *non-exporters* are defined as firms in the first two levels of export development, distinguished by their intention to engage in export operations, and *exporters* are those in the next two levels of export development, identified by their levels of export intensity

The empirical investigation in this study consists of three phases. The first step is undertaking a descriptive analysis of survey data based on descriptive statistics, correlation analyses, independent sample t-tests, and non-parametric tests to test for significant differences in the particular organisational and managerial determinants of the different stages of a firm's export development process. The second step involves performing multivariate analysis of confirmatory factor analysis to group constructs into factors influencing export development, intensity and propensity. The third step involves running a structural equation model to determine which determinants have significant effects on export development, intensity and propensity of manufacturing SMEs in Indonesia.

1.5 Organisation of the Study

The study consists of six chapters. Chapter 2 provides a critical review of theoretical and empirical studies that focus on internal determinants of export activity. This chapter also discusses the export behavioural model of the firm and the internationalisation stages of export development of SMEs. Chapter 3 discusses the methodological framework adopted in the analysis of internal determinants of export development of Indonesian manufacturing SMEs. This chapter formalises the model empirically and discusses the sources of and methods used to compile the data for the analysis. Chapter 4 presents and discusses the results of the descriptive analysis of organisational and managerial characteristics of manufacturing SMEs in Indonesia. Chapter 5 reports and discusses the causal relationships between managerial and organisational characteristics and export development. Chapter 6 summarises the empirical results, concludes, and draws several implications of the empirical results for policy formulation and implementation in the manufacturing SME sector in Indonesia.

Figure 1.1: Chapters Outline

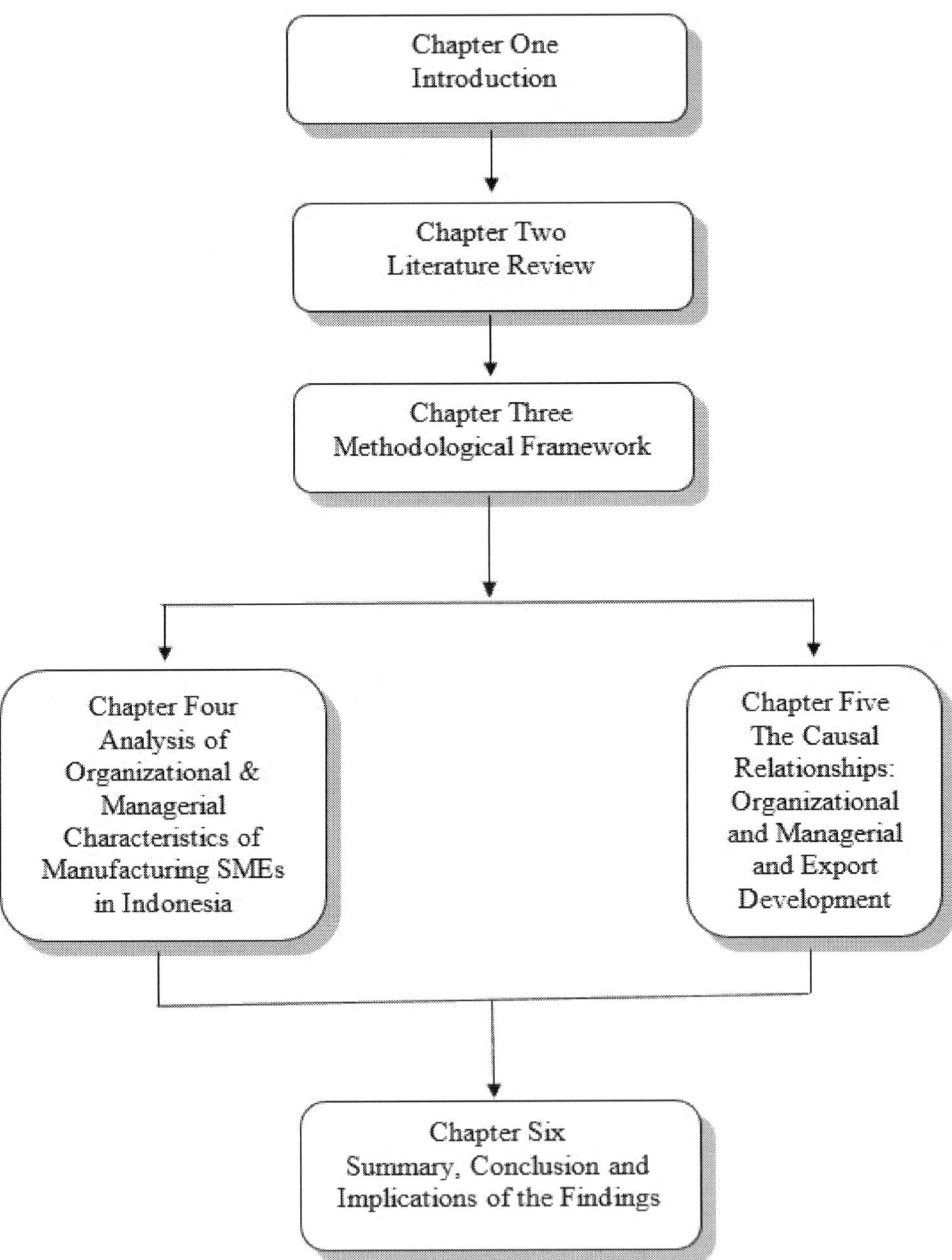

CHAPTER TWO

LITERATURE REVIEW

2.1 Introduction

Over the last decade, exporting has been one of the fastest growing economic activities, with a growth rate that exceeded the growth of world economic output (World Bank website, 2018). Exports, in 2017, accounted for about 36.95 per cent of world gross domestic product (World Bank, 2018). This demonstrates the vital role of exporting in the global economy and its contribution is likely to expand as markets become more integrated.

The significant economic improvement that can be achieved through external trade has made export development a very important field for both public and corporate policy-makers. Export endeavour is developed on the premise that it results in benefits to all participants (while acknowledging that it may create competition amongst them), regardless of whether they are nations or individual firms. For the individual firm, this usually means that profits are realized, either directly as in the case of the exporter or indirectly for the buyer who imports inputs into production. Above all, exports allow firms to capitalize on a competitive advantage, increase capacity utilisation, and raise technological standards which lead to better financial positions (Czinkota and Ronkainen, 2001; Julian and O'Cass 2004; Terpstra and Sarathy, 2000). At the national level, the benefits of exporting are determined by the impact on aggregate consumption and production. Since no country is entirely self-sufficient in terms of its ability to satisfy the whole range of the ever-changing desires of its people, international trade allows for the exploitation of competitive advantage in production and maximisation of consumption possibilities in exchange. Beyond that, exporting can improve foreign exchange reserves, provide employment, and create backward and forward linkages which eventually lead to a higher standard of living (Czinkota et al., 1992; Ahmed et al., 2006).

Despite these expected benefits, many exporting firms, particularly those in developing countries, have not optimally utilized their capacity to expand their operation in international markets. This brings up the question as to what role firms and managerial factors play in the export decision making process and the export behaviour of the firm.

The aim of this chapter is to provide a theoretical platform for the analysis of the two important constructs evident in the exporting literature: managerial and firms characteristics of a firm and export involvement. The chapter reviews key concepts, models, and elements of the macro and micro bases for international trade and exporting. By integrating insights from established theory in economics and export behaviour models, the chapter will develop a distinctive model examining the relationship between managerial and organisational characteristics and export involvement of Indonesian manufacturing SMEs. The chapter begins by providing definitions generally used by East Asian countries to classify SMEs. Next, the chapter discusses global trends that are relevant with SMEs development. It then reviews classical and alternative theories of international trade. After describing the theoretical platforms, the chapter provides an overview of export behaviour models; empirical studies in the exporting area; and models that map the relationship between managerial and organisational characteristics and export involvement of Indonesian manufacturing SMEs. Finally, the chapter concludes in Section 2.7.

2.2 Definition of SMEs

There are inconsistent definitions and classifications of SMEs being used amongst the various government agencies globally. Statistics Indonesia, for instance, defines firms with four or fewer workers as belonging to household or cottage industries; those with 5 to 19 workers are seen as small-scale enterprises; and those with 20 to 99 workers are medium-scale enterprises. Another definition is based on the value of firm assets and is generally used by "Kementerian Perindustrian" or Indonesian Ministry of Industry (abbreviated herein, henceforth KEMENPERIN) to categorize manufacturing SMEs. Firms with assets of less than 200 million rupiah are small-scale enterprises and those with assets of 200 million to 5 billion rupiah are medium scale enterprises. An additional definition is based on Indonesia's Small Business Law of 1995 which defines firms with assets (excluding land and buildings) of less than 200 million or with sales of less than 1 billion rupiah as belonging to small-scale enterprises. This definition is also used by the Central Bank of Indonesia, and by the Indonesian Ministry of Cooperatives and Small & Medium Enterprises.

Despite these inconsistencies, an alternative view supports flexibility in definition and suggests there is room for evolution. Within this view, SME-related policies are developed and customized in conjunction with the changes that are taking place in domestic and international market operations.

Table 2.1 Definition of Manufacturing SMEs in some ASEAN Countries

Economy	Definition of SMEs	
	Small	Medium
Brunei Darussalam	6-50 employees	51-100 employees
Indonesia	50 million IDR < a ≤ 500 million IDR; 300 million IDR < t ≤ 2.5 billion IDR	500 million IDR < a ≤ 2.5 billion IDR; 2.5 billion IDR < t ≤ 50 billion IDR
Malaysia	5-50 employees in manufacturing; 5-19 in agriculture and services	51-150 employees in manufacturing; 20-50 employees in agriculture and services.
Philippines	10-99 employees above Php 3 million to Php 15 million	100-199 employees above Php 15 million to Php 100 million
Singapore	< 200 employee or 100 million SGD	
Thailand	<50 employees in production, services; <25 employees in wholesale; <15 employees in retail	<200 employees in production, services; <50 employees in wholesale; <30 employees in retail
Vietnam	100-200 employees or c < 200 billion VND in agriculture, construction; 10-50 employees or c < 10 billion VND in trade and services.	200-300 employees or c < 100 billion VND in agriculture, construction; 50-100 employees or c < 50 billion VND in trade and services.

Source: IFC (2016). MSME Country Indicator.
OECD (2013). *Financing SME and Entrepreneurs 2013: An OECD scoreboard.*

Table 2.1 shows that other countries tend to use employment size, assets value, and invested capital to discriminate between SMEs and LEs (Large Enterprises).

The employment size ranges from 100 to 300 workers for SMEs. The assets value and invested capital measures vary from country to country, depending on their contribution to the economic growth and employment within single countries and depending on the business sector concerned. Thus there is no universal determinant or criteria of an SME. Much depend on the character of the relevant host country, and the profile of its own particular corporate sector, from which a relative measure of an SME is then typically made, sometimes on a rather arbitrary basis. Nevertheless, taking into account this diversity of definitions, the labour intensive nature of Indonesia's manufacturing, and the orientation of this study, SMEs in this paper will be defined as enterprises that employ 300 workers or fewer. To justify this classification, the study will also use the assets criterion from the Bank of Indonesia to validate the size of employment. Note that this definition will permit analysis of Indonesia's "missing middle" (Hayashi, 2002:24), that is the group of firms who receive the least incentives from the Indonesian government but potentially can improve Indonesia's export performance in foreign markets the most.

2.3 Global Trends in SMEs Development

For the last five decades, the role of large firms has clearly led the world economy (Down, 2010). The history of industrial economics is filled with descriptions of the growth and strategies of large size corporations that have come to dominate sectors and expand into oligopolies or monopolies. Competition only took place between a few large firms in highly concentrated markets or, in some sectors there were standalone players that controlled the whole supply to consumers within the market. This structure, to a large extent, supports the industrial pyramid which is common in every economy. The head of the pyramid usually consists of a few large enterprises and a large number of SMEs form the base (Scherer and Ross, 1990). This basic industrial structure prevails both for economically backward and advanced countries. Thus, since SMEs will continue to be numerically the larger fraction of enterprises within any economy at all times, every government is required to design prudent policies in order to assist and support these small players.

Policy assistance for SMEs, in the past, has been muted due to perceived shortcomings in the capabilities of small firms; however, this reluctance cannot be fully justified. Over time, it is evident that the role of SMEs has remained substantial and in some cases these enterprises have grown and become giant companies. Almost every big company began as an SME. Some reputable big companies, such as Microsoft for instance, started as a couple of guys in a small garage in North America; Vodafone begun as a small subsidiary from Racal; and even Volkswagen was once a small car maker in Germany. Much of this development is recorded to show that SMEs are in fact a 'seedbed' (Berry et al., 2001) for large enterprises.

SMEs substantial role in the process of industrialisation of an economy can be evidenced by their being the largest number of industrial units in both developed and developing countries and their significant contribution to total export and employment. These achievements result from SMEs' active participation in income growth, entrepreneurial training, creation of technological capabilities and job creation. Their activities have also promoted lower wage inequality and dispersion of industry away from urban areas and into regional development. As a group SMEs are also characterised by greater flexibility to changing market circumstances. (Little et al., 1987; Berry, 1992, Humphrey & Schmitz, 1996; Liedholm and Mead, 1999; Strange and Katrak, 2002). Evidence within APEC member countries in 2016, for instance, suggests that despite the whole issue of scale, there were about 19.5 million SMEs which help contribute an average 67 per cent of employment across economies (APEC, 2016). The majority of APEC economies have high percentage share of SMEs, ranging from 1.1 per cent to 57 per cent (see Table 2.2). The share and contribution to employment national economy were lower in countries such as New Zealand and Russia. Indonesia was the only country that had a very low share of SMEs at only 1.1 per cent of the total number of firms that contributed only 92 per cent of the total employment.

Table 2.2: The SMEs' Share of the Total Number of Firms and Employment (%) in APEC nations

Member Economy and Year Joined	Micro	SMEs	
	Share of Firms	Share of Firms	Share of Employment
Australia (1989)	63.2	36.8	-
Brunei Darussalam (1989)	43	57.0	58
Canada (1989)	75.5	24.6	90
Chile (1994)	90.4	8.4	80
China (1991)	0	100	75
Indonesia (1989)	98.9	1.1	92
Japan (1989)	61.1	38.9	66
Korea (1989)	86.6	13.3	87
Malaysia (1989)	74.9	22.4	57
Mexico (1993)	95.5	3.8	67
New Zealand (1989)	81.1	18.9	43
Peru (1998)	98.1	1.8	62
Philippines (1989)	92.3		61
Russia (1998)	85.0		25
Singapore (1989)	100.0		70
Chinese Taipei (1991)	97.64		78
Thailand (1989)	0	100	84
United States (1989)	78.8	21.2	56
Viet Nam (1998)	65.7	29.6	77

Notes: - = Not Available
Source: APEC (2016). SMEs in APEC Region (Infographic).

The shares of employment reported in Table 2.2 exhibit substantial difference. Countries such as Canada, Korea, and Thailand had second highest SMEs' share of employment than other APEC members with 90, 87, and 84 per cents respectively. Other countries such as Japan, China, and Chile had medium to high SMEs' share ranging between 61 per cent and 80 per cent. Despite these differences, there is a strong evidence to suggest that capitalizing on national markets and their international expansion could lead SMEs to become an engine of export growth and upgrading, particularly in developing countries (Wignaraja, 2003).

Using APEC as a point of reference, the statistics indicate that although SMEs' contribution to exports varies across countries, SMEs from developing countries were active players in the export endeavours (see for example Berry and Nugent, 1999, Tambunan et al., 2007, Wignaraja and O'Neil in Lall, 1999) and they tend to invest in younger industries rather than more mature ones (Acs and Preston, 1997). Yet, since SMEs were using various modes of entry in their export endeavours, including indirect modes of sub-contracting or marketing relationships, their contributions to total exports were often excluded from official statistics. By improving their quality, price, and delivery, a few SMEs made significant progress and were able to survive and even establish their own label in overseas markets. It is estimated that the export value of SMEs make up anywhere between 15 per cent and 70 per cent of the total export value of a given economy. The highest export value of SMEs as a share of total export value is owned by China; followed by Canada and Korea (less than 50 per cent); Thailand and Vietnam (less than 35 per cent); Indonesia, Japan Malaysia, Singapore and the United States (less than 25 per cent); and Australia and Chile (less than 15 per cent) (Source: APEC, 2016)

The rapid expansion of the global market economy, which is underpinned by technological progress in communication and transportation and systemic synchronisation through economic integration, is likely to open up many opportunities for SMEs around the world, including Indonesia. Despite the different viewpoints on the implications of globalisation for SMEs in developing countries, the significant changes in the size and structure of developing country exports is evidence of an increasing integration of the international environment. These current economic realities are likely to improve if a dynamic SME sector increases its participation in international trade and appropriate policies maintain their support for sustainable exports from SMEs.

2.4 A Review of Theoretical Studies

The fundamental rationales that move the wheels of trade among countries are not as simple as those that influence trade within the national boundaries. Although it is evident that trade can bring about tremendous benefits to business firms and the nation's economy, a more comprehensive understanding can only be achieved by analysing a selected number of international trade and foreign direct investment theories. These theories offer explanations of trade flows between at least two nations, the nature and extent of gains or losses to an economy, and the effects of trade policies on an economy.

2.4.1 The Classical Theory of International Trade

One of the major concepts of international trade is absolute advantage developed by Adam Smith (1723-1790). This theory is based on the concept of economic advantage and states that countries tend to specialize in those products in which they have an absolute advantage, specifically, in terms of lower cost of production. A condition of absolute advantage exists when one country has a cost advantage (produced with fewer resources) over another country in the production of one product, while the second country has a cost advantage over the first country in producing a second product. With the assumption of a two-country and two-product world, international trade and specialisation will be beneficial to each country when the country is absolutely more efficient than its trading partner.

The absolute advantage theory is also aimed at explaining why costs differ among nations. According to the theory, productivities of factor inputs with natural advantage and/or acquired advantage, will determine the cost differences among nations. Natural advantages consist of factors relating to climate, soil, and mineral wealth, whereas acquired advantages consist of special skills, technical, and marketing know-how, and so on. With such advantages, a nation would produce that item at lower cost than a trading partner without the same advantages. The main limitation of the absolute advantage theory is in its assumption which fails to explain the situation of one country having absolute advantage in the production of both products, but still trading with another country in these products.

Another classical concept of international trade is comparative advantage formulated by David Ricardo (1772-1823). This theory argues that in order for trade to be carried on profitably, it is not necessary for a country to have an absolute advantage over other countries. If one country has an absolute advantage over another country in the production of all products, trade will be gainful if the domestic exchange ratios in each country are not similar. In other words, if the country with the absolute advantage has a greater advantage in producing one product than it has in producing another, the country will benefit by specializing in and exporting the product in which it has the greatest advantage, or superior (comparative) advantage, and importing the product in which it has less advantage. The other country, even though it is at a disadvantage in producing all products, can still benefit by specializing in and exporting the product in which it has least disadvantage. In the real world, however, the power of comparative advantage seems weaker than what its model implies. There is evidence to show that countries tend not to specialize in any product. Despite its significance, comparative advantage theory does little to explain what causes the variation in comparative costs.

2.4.2 The Factor Proportion Theory

The limitation of the comparative advantage theory is solved by the factor proportion theory which offers an explanation for the differences in comparative costs among trading nations. This theory contends that the differences in supply condition of factor productivities and factor endowments explain much of international trade. If trading nations have the same taste and preference of demands, use factors of production that are of uniform quality, and use the same technology, then productivity of a given resource unit is identical for both trading nations.

The factor proportion theory maintains that relative price levels differ among countries because: firstly, they have different relative endowments of factors of production (capital and labour inputs); and secondly, different commodities require different intensities of factor inputs in their production. In other words, countries will tend to generate and export products that require a large amount of the relatively abundant or cheap input, and will import a product which uses the relatively expensive input in their production. This theory, therefore, extends the concept of economic advantage by considering the endowments and costs of factors of production. The fundamental explanation of the pattern of international trade rests on the uneven distribution of world resources among nations, coupled with the reality that products require different proportions of the factors of production. When a country possesses a great amount of resources required to produce a product, its price for that product will be low compared with its price for another product requiring great amounts of scarcer resources.

The empirical test carried out in the United States of America by Leontief (1953), however, showed a contradictory result. As a capital abundant country, the United Stated would be expected to export capital-intensive goods, but the facts revealed that the USA exported labour intensive goods and imported capital-intensive products. This inconsistency can be explained by the human skill in labour-intensive production which was not taken into account. Corden (1994) argues that the factor proportion theory only mentions the proportions between labour and capital and does not take into consideration skilled labour intensity, technology intensity, and human capital intensity. The same input requirement, therefore, does not simply imply the same factor intensities because the composition of value added might be different from each of the factor inputs.

2.4.3 The Product Life-cycle Theory

Rapid technological progress and the development of multinational enterprises since the 1960s have caused the earlier trade theories, which were based on the economic advantage of factor endowments, to become obsolete. There was then a need to search for an alternative international trade theory that suited the changing realities of the evolving commercial realm. The product life-cycle (PLC) theory developed by Vernon (1966) explained not only the trade patterns of manufacturers but also multinational expansion of sales and production subsidiaries.

According to this theory, many manufactured goods particularly technologically advanced products, experience a trade cycle. The process, which consists of various stages, starts with the introduction stage when the innovator company establishes a technological innovation in the production of manufactured goods. Initially, the relatively small home market and not fully developed technological efficiency may hinder the company in achieving mass economies of scale in production.

In the next stage of growth and expansion, the innovator begins to export its product to foreign markets with relatively similar tastes, income levels, and demand structures. The larger the market becomes and the more efficient the technology, the greater the capacity of the company to switch to mass-production operation and increase the amount of goods to be supplied in the world market.

As time passes and the technology becomes more common place in the foreign market, the domestic company finds it necessary to move its production operation closer to the foreign market in order to protect its foreign sales and export profits. This stage is recognized as mature when the conditions change due to the fact that the cost advantage enjoyed by the innovator from the outset is not likely to last forever.

Although the innovating country's monopoly position may be lengthened by legal rights such as patents and other intellectual property rights, this often decreases over a period of time. Foreign producers may begin to imitate the production process and the innovating country may start to lose its comparative advantage and its export cycle then enters the declining stage. The cycle is complete when the technology becomes very common and homogeneous such that it can be applied by all nations anywhere in the world. Thus, due to increasing foreign competition, the innovating country may end up becoming a net importer of the product from a place where the costs of production are the lowest (Vernon, 1966, 1979).

The main factors in explaining patterns of international trade, according to this theory, are technological innovation and market expansion (Morgan and Katsikeas, 1997). The main limitation of this theory is in its insufficient explanation of the competitive processes that accompany the market expansion. Lambkin and Day (1989) set out some of the specific limitations. First, the theory overlooks the presence and behaviour of substitutes. The declining stage of a life cycle is often hastened by an emerging substitute with a new basis of comparative advantage. Second, the theory also ignores differences between large and small firms, between established and new firms, between firms that develop their own entry and those that enter the market by acquisition, licensing, or joint venture, or between firms that choose to follow different strategies. Third, the simple one-way establishment of the birth-life-death analogy can be misleading due to some evidence of successful strategies to rejuvenate and extend life cycles by sustaining marketing and R & D investments which in turn will protect the innovator's market share position. Fourth, it fails to recognize the important role of government and a favourable regulatory environment to legitimize the new industry.

2.4.4 New Trade Theories and its Principles

The conceptual limitations of the standard trade theories which were built on the assumption of perfect competition, free trade, and unregulated trade, suggest that it is imperative to consider trade theories that are not constrained by these assumptions.

The new trade theories began to emerge in the 1970s when a number of economists were questioning the assumption of diminishing returns to specialisation used in international trade theory. They argued that increasing returns to specialisation might exist in some industries. This section explains some of the important sources of increasing returns by largely focusing on the rise of intra-industry trade, economies of scale and market imperfection (Krugman and Obstfeld, 2003).

2.4.4.1 Intra-industry Trade

Comparative advantage theory suggests that nations with similar production-side capabilities (and relatively similar general demand patterns) should trade little with each other. Industrialized countries with relatively similar factor of endowments (physical capital, skilled labour, unskilled labour, technology, and technological capabilities), therefore, should trade rather little with each other, except in the case of primary products where differences in endowments of productive land and natural resources are significant.

In reality, industrialized countries trade extensively with each other in what is called intra-industry trade. Over 70 per cent of the exports of industrialized countries go to other industrialized countries (NAPES, 2004). Intra-industry trade is the international trade of products made within the same industry such as steel-for-steel, or bread-for-bread (Gerber, 2005). This increasing phenomenon, as argued by Grimwade (2000), cannot be explained within the framework of classical trade theory and has encouraged researchers to look at other explanations. Several attempts to explain and measure this trade were carried out by Grubel and Lloyd (1975), Tharakan (1983), Greenaway and Tharakan (1986), Greenaway and Milner (1986), and Vona (1991).

Much of intra-industry trade involves trade in differentiated products, or exports and imports of different varieties of the same basic product or the same industry. Part of the reason for the rise of intra-industry trade, according to Pugel and Lindert (2000) is that product variety is considered a luxury in advanced countries. The demand for luxuries is rising even faster due to the increasing per capita incomes occurring in these economies. The higher the incomes of consumers, the more consumers can seek variety in the products that they buy. Thus, prosperous people vary their choices of wines, automobiles, clothing and so on. But, the increasing demand by itself cannot explain the intra industry trade trend. In order to put intra-industry trade in a clear perspective, it is necessary to consider the characteristics on the producer's side of the same expanding markets. At this point moderate internal economies of scale and monopolistic competition come into play in explaining this phenomenon.

2.4.4.2 Economies of Scale

Economies of scale or increasing returns to scale exist if increasing expenditures on all inputs (with input prices constant) increase the output quantity by a larger percentage so that the average cost of producing each unit of output declines (Pugel and Lindert, 2000). Intra-industry trade is driven by the desire for differentiated products and the production of any one particular variety of product requires some fixed costs. Thus, the more the Mercedes-Benz convertibles are produced, for instance, the lower the unit cost. The role of scale economies allows each country to specialize in producing a restricted range of goods which leads to more efficient production as an alternative to producing everything for itself. This advantage and trade with each other enables each country to consume the full range of goods (Krugman and Obstfeld, 2003).

The model of trade based on economies of scale, however, promotes market structures other than perfect competition. The concept of economies of scale may be either externally or internally propelled. When the cost per unit depends on the size of the industry and not on the size of any one firm, then the economies of scale are said to be externally driven. When the cost per unit depends on the size of an individual firm and not necessarily on that of the industry, then economies of scale are said to be internally driven.

2.4.4.3 Imperfect Competition

Another point of departure from comparative advantage trade theory is caused by the absence of highly competitive international markets. Some important industries in the world are controlled by a few large firms. Commercial aircraft, for instance, is dominated by Boeing and Airbus. Microprocessor production is controlled by Intel and Motorola. The standard model, therefore, may not be appropriate to analyse such industries as the assumption of perfect competition has been violated as these industries move toward global oligopolies. One key explanation of such occurrences is that the exploitation of scale economies, according to Pugel and Lindert (2000), determine why a few firms reach the most efficient level of production and dominate some industries.

Imperfect competition prevails in any market where the producers or consumers have market power to influence prices. Several forms of imperfect competition are found in the literature, including: 1) Monopolistic competition - where there is a relatively large number of small producers or suppliers offering similar, but not identical products. If perfect competition requires the presence of hundreds or thousands of firms, monopolistic competition only needs a fairly large number, such as 25, 35 or 60. Firms have a limited amount of control over market price. Unlike perfect competition that is characterised by a standardized product, monopolistic competition has the fundamental feature of product differentiation. Therefore despite the presence of a relatively large number of firms, monopolistically competitive producers do have some control over the prices of their products; 2) Oligopoly – where there are a small number of firms that are attracted into markets by high profits but where entry is restricted by barriers. Firms in this structure are characterized by internal economies of scale and the industry is comprised of a few large firms that have the ability to affect prices but none have the market power of uncontested monopoly.

The opportunity for a large number of firms to participate in an industry will increase if the scale economies are modest and moderate. If, in addition, products are differentiated in quality, sales, installation services, location and so on, then there will be opportunities for imperfect competition of the monopolistic competition kind. If scale economies are substantial over a large range of output, then a few firms are likely to grow to be large in order reap the scale economies. If a few large firms control the global industry, then the industry can be said to be oligopolistic.

Thus new trade theories suggest that even in the absence of factor advantages, firms are able to gain cost advantages that will allow them to export. The focus on differences in tastes and preferences and product differentiation in new trade theories can also explain trade in similar goods.

2.4.5 The Competitive Advantage of Nations

One of many explanations for differences in intra-industry performance is the competitive advantage theory. Michael Porter (1990) in this theory maintains that the success of a nation in a particular industry, and thus in an international arena, is invented and is not inherited from its traditional factor endowments, its labour pool, its interest rate, or its currency's value as maintained by classical or factor proportions theories of trade. Porter noted that a nation's competitiveness depends on the ability of its industry to innovate and upgrade. Through the pressure and the challenge of competition in the market, for example, companies can learn and invent a way to cope with strong domestic rivals, aggressive home based suppliers, and demanding local customers.

The role of a nation, according to this theory, is to encourage the creation of an environment that fosters innovation and the absorption of knowledge into the goods and services being traded. The inimitable characteristics owned by a nation, such as culture, national values, economic structures, and histories, play a crucial role in determining its competitive position. Porter's theory further maintained that these differences lead to a distinctive direction of competitiveness in every country. This distinctiveness, which represents the restrictedness of every home environment, however, also produces an inability of every nation to become competitive in every industry.

In describing the approach that gains success in international markets, Porter concludes that companies with international leadership typically employ distinctive strategies relative to their competitors but fundamentally move in the same path of operation. Through experiences, companies usually identify a new basis for competing or find better methods for competing in old ways. These improvements can be manifested in a new product design, a new production process, a new marketing approach, or a new way of conducting training. The majority of these ideas, however, are not original ideas. They are usually pre-existing ideas that have never been followed up intensively.

In discussing the pattern of national competitive success, Porter uses the study carried out in the ten trading nations to distinguish national competitive advantage from idiosyncratic advantage. Some measures of competitive advantage used in the study are the existence of extensive and continuous exports to other nations and/or substantial foreign investment based on skills and assets created in the home country. Based on the findings, it is concluded that successful companies tend to develop a predisposition for certainty and stability. They are inclined to pursue improvements by seeking an increasingly complex source of competitive advantage. They also have the capabilities to solve problems associated with change and innovation.

Porter noted that the above tendencies are strongly influenced by the four determinants that shape the diamond of national advantage (Porter, 1990), which are:

1. Factor conditions. In examining the factor conditions, Porter's theory goes beyond the traditional factors of land, labour and capital by including the quality of the work force (skilled labour) and the quality of individual infrastructure necessary to compete in a given industry.
2. Demand conditions. In reviewing the demand conditions, Porter notes that the existence of large and sophisticated home-market demand helps, in that firms that can survive and flourish in the highly competitive home markets tend to gain a competitive edge as they have a clearer and earlier picture of emerging buyer needs and faster response to innovation requirements.

3. Related and supporting industries. The presence or absence of the nation's supplier industries and other related industries are critical for the production, marketing and distribution needs of a firm. A firm that is operating within a pool of related firms and industries gains advantages of close working relationships, proximity to suppliers, and timeliness of product and information flows (Czinkota et al, 2003).
4. Firm strategy, structure, and rivalry. This pertains to the conditions in the home market governing how companies are created, organized, and managed, as well as the nature of domestic rivalry. Porter noted that firms facing intense competition in the domestic market are drilled through costs, quality, productivity and innovation to survive; the elements which are also needed in international markets.

The above determinants together with all other necessary variables, such as the availability of resources and skills required in an industry; the information that shapes the opportunities that companies perceive; the directions in which they develop their resources and skills; the goals of the owners, managers, and individuals in companies; and the pressures on companies to invest and innovate, determine the fulfilment of international competitive advantage. Porter also maintains that firms are most likely to succeed in industries or industry segments where the sources of competitive advantage are more favourable; an important point which justifies the importance of the industry structure not only in directing the investment activities of firms but also in creating pressures for innovation through intensive domestic rivalry.

In addition, Porter includes two other exogenous variables that can influence the national system in important ways. These are chance and government. Chance is defined as "occurrences that have little to do with circumstances in a nation and are often largely outside the power of firms (and often the national government) to influence" (Porter, 1990, page 124). According to Porter:

> "chance events are important because they create discontinuities that allow shifts in competitive position. They can nullify the advantages previously established competitors held and create the potential that a new nation's firm can supplant them to achieve competitive advantage in response to new and different conditions." (Porter, 1990, page 124).

Some examples of chance events are: acts of pure invention, major technological discontinuities (biotechnology, microelectronics), discontinuities in input costs such as the oil shocks, significant shifts in world financial markets or exchange rates, surges of world or regional demand, political decisions by foreign governments, or wars (Porter, 1990, page 124). Unexpected shifts in any of these issues can become a force to generate new mechanisms to cope with selective factor disadvantages.

While most of the previously reviewed theories do not visit the role of the government in their analysis, Porter justified the role for the government at all levels. Government, as stated by Porter, can improve (or detract from) the national advantage of the nations by influencing the four determinants of competitive advantage. Government's new regulations and policies, for example, can change the previous home demand and factor conditions.

Porter's theory has spawned a number of inquiries that are the focus of debate. One of these is the meaning and measurement of 'competitiveness' or 'competitive advantage' and the relationship between the competitiveness of an economy and that of the industries and firms that operate within it. Although studies such as

Sagebien (1990) declare Porter's definition of competitiveness as a breakthrough as it equates with national productivity, other studies such as Eilon (1990) argue that this proposition is confusing and misleading. Productivity, according to Eilon, is different from competitiveness, as one is an efficiency measure of resources use while the other refers to competency in gaining market share. This explanation clarifies why Porter's theory does not offer guidance on how competitive advantage should be defined and measured.

The term of competitiveness or productivity of a nation was also examined by Clark (1991) who provided evidence that this term was not actually similar to the competitiveness of its industries. Porter (1990) asserted that the competitiveness or productivity of a nation is essentially the competitiveness or productivity of any industries located in that country. Evidence such as Japanese auto-makers that established factories in Britain and outperformed local firms by using the same factors of production or American electronic companies that gained a high level of productivity in other countries (Reich, 1990), have shed a light on the difference between the national and industrial context of productivity. Porter argued that a nation is essentially an aggregation of industries and its economic performance is determined by the competitiveness of those industries for which it is the home base and the appropriate level of analysis should therefore be the industry. Congdon (1990) maintained that this description confounds the context of analysis of nation, industry and firm levels.

From the above accounts, it can be concluded that Porter's theory represents a combination of the distinguishing characteristics of comparative advantage and new trade theory. Hill (2002) noted that if Porter's theory is right, then a country's export pattern needs to reflect the presence of the four main components mentioned in the diamond model. Furthermore, countries will import goods from industries where some or all the components are missing domestically. The extent to which Porter's theory can explain many aspects of internationalisation at the firm level, however, remains limited, since the basis of Porter's diamond model is the nation/industry level of analysis. His emphasis on industry level was reflected in his explanation of each industry's diamond that captures the relative attractiveness of each particular industry. Porter (1990), in addition, attempted to identify a nation's 'competitive' industries and measured them based on their export-share statistics. Although, this measurement was considered flawed, for it was measuring companies located in the nation regardless of their home base, it is clear that the focus of measurement was the industry within a nation. Thus, Porter's theory is incapable of explaining differences that may exist at the individual firm level, and it is necessary to extend the analysis to other relevant export theories to explain factors affecting firm's engagement in international markets.

2.5 A Review of Empirical Studies - Export Behavioural Models

In contrast to the international theories as presented earlier, export behaviour models attempt to explain *why* and *how* individual firms engage in export activities as part of the internationalisation process, and how the dynamic nature of such activities can be conceptualized. Export behaviour is defined both as the probability of being an exporter and export intensity for the exporting firm (Wakelin 1998, Basile, 2001). The focus is explicitly on determinants of export engagement. Perceived export benefits, perceived export barriers, firm size, and managerial characteristics are among important determinants found in export behaviour. Companies engaging in foreign marketing activities are often driven by the firm's expectations relative to their short term and long term objectives but they usually lack prior knowledge, experience, marketing information, and so on, which hinders their ability to initiate, develop, or sustain business operations in overseas markets.

2.5.1 Internal Determinants of Export Development

To act as an engine of development, international trade through exports must lead to steady improvements in managerial and organisational skillls by developing performance at individual, team, and organisational levels. From this perspective, exports and a country's development cannot be seen simply as the aggregate of its economic growth and export performance. Exports represent a synthesis of the interaction between people's choices and trade with a view to improve their living standards, particularly through export engagement. The extent of such choice, in turn, depends on the interplay between internal and external factors that determine export outcome.

Several empirical studies have attempted to provide a quantitative indication of export behaviour by systematically accounting for factors governing export behaviour. Reviews by Bilkey (1978), Miesenbock (1988), Aaby and Slater (1989), Chetty and Hamilton (1993), Leonidou and Katsikeas (1996), Zou and Stan (1998), and Coviello and McAuley (1999) are those that are mostly cited in the literature. The empirical studies have included a wide range of industries for their analysis including the services industry. Most of the studies, however, dealt with SMEs from developed countries with only a few from newly industrialized and developing countries.

A substantial body of literature on this subject had been developed as early as the 1960's (see Mintz, 1967). But the fragmented nature of the research and the lack of consensus on the findings, have meant that the field suffers from a lack of proper synthesis and assimilation (Leonidou and Katsikeas, 1996). Despite this growing critique, a careful review of these empirical studies suggests that combination and interaction between external and internal factors (Leonidou, 2004; Aaby and Slater, 1989; Brooks and Rosson, 1982) plays a complementary role in influencing export behaviour and can lead to the direction of change over time, including to initiate or withdrawal from exports.

Unlike Porter's theory that included "entrepreneurship" as an inseparable factor in the diamond framework, most of the empirical research above was carried out explicitly seeking the relevant attributes that distinguish exporters from non-exporters and identifying the attributes correlating with success in exporting. A number of decision maker's characteristics are highlighted in the export behaviour literature and, as per Suarez-ortega and Alamo-vera (2005), include:

1) Age group
2) Level of education
3) International experience
4) Knowledge of foreign language
5) Professional and general business experience

Source: Suarez-ortega, Alamo-vera, 2005.

Manager's age – Manager's age has been studied as a predictor of differences between exporting and non exporting firms. The proposed assumption built on this characteristic is that younger managers tend to be more internationally minded and cosmopolitan than older managers (Leonidou et al., 1998). The results from a number of studies, however, show mixed conclusions. Ross (1989), Tseng and Yu (1991), Ursic and Czinkota (1989), and Dichtl et al. (1990), for example, found that younger managers are more enthusiastic about innovations such as exporting than older managers.

Other studies, however, show that managers in older age are associated with firm internationalisation (see for example Westhead, 1995). Philp and Wickramasekera (1995), Brooks and Rosson (1982), Davis and Harveston (2000), and Suarez-

Ortega and Alamo-Vera (2005) found that there were no significant age differences between the managers in exporting companies and the ones in non-exporting companies.

Manager's level of education – Manager's level of education has been highlighted by Keng and Jiuan's study (1989). Based on their research on exporting and non-exporting firms in Singapore, it is found that the majority of exporting managers (around 40 per cent) have received graduate and postgraduate education against 6 per cent in non-exporting firms. They also found that the higher the education of the chief executive officers among the exporting firms, the greater was the degree of involvement. A study by Wood and Jordan (2000) emphasized that managers with higher levels of education might be more likely to have contacts abroad, especially if they obtained their degrees overseas and might be willing to overcome bureaucratic barriers to exporting. Studies that have shown a positive relationship between education level and export behaviour are Aggrey et al. (2010), Suarez-Ortega and Alamo-Vera (2005), Wood and Jordan (2000), and Holzmuller and Kasper (1990). The study that showed no significant differences between exporters and non-exporters in their level of education was that carried out by Brooks and Rosson (1982).

Manager's international experience – Manager's international experience is considered important because it helps a firm to have a direct encounter with the international market's opportunities and threats. This factor was mostly measured by international travel and time spent abroad/residence abroad.

Several studies that have found a positive relationship between international experience and the level of export involvement are those carried out by Fischer and Reuber (2003), Ibeh and Young (2001), Schlegelmilch and Ross (1987), Da Rocha et al. (1990), Barret and Wilkinson (1986), and Garniers (1982). Managers, who have the experience of travelling overseas, are more likely to learn about foreign business practices, meet prospective customers, and identify market opportunities than those who do not (Da Rocha et al., 1990). Cavusgil and Naor's (1987) and Moon and Lee's (1990) studies, however, show no significant relationship between the manager's international experience and the firm's export development level.

Manager's knowledge of foreign language – Manager's knowledge of foreign language has been highlighted by Burton and Schlegelmilch's (1987), Dichtl et al. (1990), Holzmuller and Kasper (1991) and Leonidou et al. (1998). Based on their findings, it is concluded that foreign languages are antecedents of attitude towards exports. Managers with good command of foreign languages will be able to establish social contacts and networks, to understand the ethos and business practices of a market, to improve communication to and from a market, and to improve the ability to negotiate and interact with foreign customers.

Other studies in New Zealand showed that export success is positively related to the employment of a foreign language specialist (see Enderwick and Akoorie, 1994; Stanley et al., 1989). The Daniels and Guyburo (1976) study, found significant differences only for the English language and concluded that only the knowledge of English is meaningful for export involvement as it is widely used in international business.

Other internal factors are sourced from the **organisational characteristics of the firm**. The most common organisational attributes found in the literature are:

1) Size of a firm
2) Distinctive capabilities
3) Experience in geographic market development
4) Age of a firm

5) Location in the domestic market

Size of a firm – Size of a firm has been the most researched variable in firms' export behaviour literature (Zou and Stan, 1998). The justification is based on the four advantages that their size grants to large firms that makes them more efficient in terms of exporting (Leonidou, 1998). Firstly, large firms, in general, have more financial, human and material resources available, which are necessary in maintaining and developing an export programs (Cavusgil and Naor, 1987). Secondly, their managers usually are more competent and dynamic, and recognize the importance of developing an effective strategy to exports (Tookey, 1964). Size, therefore facilitates entry into an export market and allows greater ability to respond to the foreign customers' demand effectively (Katsikeas et al., 1995). Thirdly, large firms tend to be more competitive than their small counterparts due to their ability to create more scale economies and having greater power in the market (Samiee and Walters, 1990). Finally, since large firms usually have easier access to sources of information, they tend to have greater tolerance toward risk and ability to withstand the impact of international breakdowns (Bonaccorsi, 1992; Balabanis and Katsikea, 2003). The most common criterion used to measure the size of a firm is number of full time employees. Other criteria include annual sales volume, and the value of the assets of a firm.

According to Sterlacchini (2001), the direct effect of size is not significant for exports, as exporting requires fewer resources compared with other forms of entry into international markets (Bonaccorsi, 1992). Rather, the relationship between size and export behaviour is influenced by the strategy pursued by the company. So, if SMEs could agglomerate to have open access to information, they would be able to focus on specialized resource products for export markets. Agglomeration would also reduce SMEs' risk perceptions by copying other companies

(Bonaccorsi, 1992). SMEs' agility toward fast-changing global environments, in addition, gives them a greater flexibility and ability to adapt to changes and overcome difficulties quickly as their managerial structure and coordination systems tend to be less formal than those of large firms (Balabanis and Katsikea, 2003).

Manager's perception of firm's competitive advantage – One of the important aspects of management perception and interpretation is their view of the set of characteristics of direct competitors to the firm (Chen, 1996). Managerial perceptions of similarities and differences between their firm and competitors can be the source of information to recognize their resources and capabilities, and to respond to the rivalry through various strategies (Deephouse, 1999).

Management estimation of the firm's possession of distinctive capabilities or competitive advantages for exporting has been found to significantly impact on export involvement. Firms possessing distinctive capabilities, of either the resource or capability kind, according to Wiedersheim-Paul et al. (1978), have high motivation to become involved in export markets either through investment or trade. Since there are usually sunk costs involved in developing that competence, a firm usually allocates them extensively (Wiedersheim et al. 1978). Other studies have also supported this proposition. Katsikeas (1994b), Moon and Lee (1990), and Burton and Schlegelmilch (1987) for instance, maintained that the firm's possession of competitive advantages plays an important role in improving the willingness and preparation of the firm to initiate exporting. Lack of competitive advantage, on the contrary, may be seen as a barrier to export involvement and export success.

Age of a firm is mostly measured by the number of years the business has been in operation. Firm age can explain the extent of a firm's learning experience (Graner and Isaksson, 2002). If market forces discipline technically inefficient producers, then older firms will tend to be more competitive producers in the world markets

(Roberts and Tybout, 1997). The positive relationship between age of a firm and export business activities has been identified by Johanson and Vahlne (1977), Wiedersheim-Paul et al. (1978), Bilkey and Tesar (1977), and Welch and Wiedersheim-Paul (1980). These researchers support the view that the internationalisation of firms follows a step-wise learning process and since age is considered an accumulation of knowledge and experience, the established firms are more likely to export than the inexperienced ones.

Contrasting findings, however, were found in Aggrey et al. (2010), Clarke (2005), Tseng and Yu (1991) and Wengel and Rodriguez (2006). These studies found that younger firms are more interested in foreign operations than older ones. This is explained by the fact that the younger firms tend to perceive exporting as the only way to increase sales and achieve growth as opposed to the older firms which are often well-established in the domestic market. Other studies that have found no correlation between the firm's age and export involvement are those by Bell (1995) and Keng and Jiuan (1989).

Geographic market development has also been considered as a determinant of export behaviour. In this study it is described as expansion of the firm across areas or regions within the domestic market. It is, therefore, an indicator of domestic geographical scope which, according to the Uppsala internationalisation model, can be a head start for international market involvement. One of the basic assumptions of the Uppsala model is that the firm will grow within its domestic market before developing foreign markets (Johanson and Wiedersheim-Paul, 1975). Its presence in more distant regions allows a firm to become more familiar with obstacles and costs of communication. When these barriers are overcome, the relative foreignness of distant markets is reduced (Wiedersheim-Paul et al. 1978). In short, as the firm is gaining more skills in marketing a product at a distance, it increases its confidence to extend its communication network. Domestic market expansion, moreover, motivates firm's appreciation of the limitations of the domestic market and directs managers to foreign market opportunities (Reid, 1983). The learning and sequential perspective of the internationalisation process will then lead to the accomplishment of a higher export commitment.

Firms' location in the domestic market has been found to be an important factor that influences firm export behaviour. Based on Olson and Wiedersheim-Paul (1978) study, it is concluded that companies located near information centres or close to national borders, for example, are more likely to engage in exporting activities due to a greater exposure to various export stimuli. Close proximity to transportation points, such as ports, airports, and railway stations that link the home country with foreign markets, is also assumed to facilitate export development and performance in overseas markets due to cost effectiveness (Wiedersheim-Paul et al., 1978).

In the less advanced markets, significant geographic variations and wide discrepancies in infrastructure and economic development between urban and rural areas may impact on firms' propensity to export (Zhao and Zou, 2002). Firms in urban areas gain more advantage due to their close proximity to centres of information and various export stimuli (Dicken and Lloyd, 1990; Knight and Gappert, 1989, Wiedersheim-Paul et al. 1978; Zhao and Zou, 2002), than those found in rural areas. This, in turn can improve the chances that other businesses will survive and succeed (Mittelstaedt et al. 2006).

2.5.2 External Determinants of Export Development

In addition to the internal determinants that are associated with the decision-maker and organisational attributes of the firm, there are external determinants or those factors that originate from outside the organisational boundaries of the individual firm and which cannot be easily and directly controlled by them. External determinants of export behaviour are usually conceptualized as obstacles or barriers to exporting (Gripsurd, 1990).

A critical review of the export literature, however, shows that there are only a few studies that have set out to empirically examine the relationship between external variables and the firm's export behaviour. The complexity and the dynamism of each element of the external environment is stated to be the main reason for this lack of investigation. Thus, in order to understand the impact of these determinants on the firm's decision to export, most of the studies rely on manager's perceptions as a standard of measurement. The managers' perceptions of and attitude towards environmental influences and the appropriateness of strategies to exploit them are claimed to be the major determinants of market entry mode choice, level of internationalisation and/or performance.

The analysis of external determinants to export development can be divided into main areas of domestic and foreign market environment. Yeoh in Axinn (1994) defines the domestic market environment as those uncontrollable market forces and conditions but within the home country of operations. While the foreign market environment as those uncontrollable market forces and conditions outside the firm's domestic market environment.

Domestic external determinants of export development that are frequently identified in the literature are: 1) The size and state of the domestic market and 2) Export promotion program. While foreign external determinants are: 1) Level of competition; 2) Tariff barriers; 3) Non-tariff barriers; and 4) Physical and Psychological distance (*Source*: Weaver et al., 1998; Liargovas and Skandalis, 2008)

The size and state of the domestic market can be summarized using four variables: total population size and income levels/distribution; educational levels; levels of industry competition; and availability and quality of business infrastructure.

1) Population size and income levels/distribution are variables used as proxies for market size. The income level and its distribution are useful data as they indicate the market potential for both consumer and industrial products. The figures from these three variables are crucial in evaluating the size of the market available to a firm

Domestic markets that fail to provide adequate economies of scale and scope are seen by Czinkota and Ursic (1991) as providing the common trigger for a firm to initiate exports. A study by Kaynak and Kothari (1984) shows that the most common reason found in non-exporting US firms for not exporting was the existence of plenty of opportunities in the home market. Large domestic markets, therefore, can act as an inhibitor to export development as they often provide enough demand to not warrant searching for new markets. Small domestic markets, on the contrary, can encourage firms to look outside their domestic market for increased sales and business growth.

2) Level of competition in an industry has been highlighted by Kaynak et al. (1987), Kim (1987), Morgan and Katsikeas (1997), Pavord and Bogart (1975), Sullivan and Bauerschmidt (1988), and Tsai et al. (1991). Their studies show that the attractiveness of a market depends on the intensity of competition within an industry. Once the home market conditions become so saturated, management pushes to investigate exporting in order to avoid losses and increase sales.

Increasing competition, therefore, is an important determinant of firms' intentions in penetrating foreign markets.

3) Educational level has been examined by a number of studies such as Czinkota and Ronkainen (1998), Crick and Chaudry (2000), Da Silva and Da Rocha (2001), and Leonidou (1995b). The findings confirm that educational levels do have an impact on business functions as they usually have a direct impact on the availability of skilled and unskilled labour in a population.

4) Business infrastructure in the domestic market such as transportation networks, communication infrastructure, or information and financing facilities, plays a critical role for any firm's success. Inadequate and unreliable communication infrastructure such as telephones lines and internet facilities, can impair the ability of countries to engage in international trade (Kessides, 1993). The problem of poor infrastructure is commonly found as a major barrier to business in general and international business in particular for firms operating in developing countries. This has been identified by several studies such as Ibeh and Young (2001), Ross (1989) and Bodur (1986). Physical infrastructure, therefore, functions as a public asset to support private capital in the production process.

Export promotion program is defined as all readily available external sources of information and experiential knowledge that provide the firm with an external capacity to cope with the complexities of exporting (Gencturk and Kotabe, 2001). Government export promotion programs are widely discussed in the empirical research for their role in developing awareness of opportunities and organisational capabilities, and can provide cost sharing opportunities (Seringhaus and Botschen, 1991). Several studies such as Crick and Chaudry (1997), Donthu and Kim (1993), and Katsikeas et al. (1996) revealed that export promotion programs are one of the export motivators for SMEs. Kotabe and Czinkota (1992) suggested firms with logistic-related problems, legal procedural matters and problems in developing foreign market intelligence were those that were highly affected by these assistances. The most common measures taken by government to promote exports in a country are economic cooperation/alliances with other nations or groups of nations, business-friendly macroeconomic policy, and export assistance programs.

1) Economic cooperation - Bilateral and multilateral trade agreements are examples of economic cooperation usually carried out to promote trade. Countries that become members of this cooperation are able to take advantage of reduced or abolished tariff and non-tariff trade barriers. Other advantages, as noted by Czinkota et al. (2003), include trade creation, economies of scale, improved terms of trade, reduction of monopoly power and improved cross-cultural communication. Apart from those advantages, economic integration, however, may bring about an increasing competition to local businesses.

2) Macroeconomic policy – Macroeconomic policies are usually pursued by government and include policy measures on exchange rates, availability of finance, inflation and tax.

(i) *Exchange rate* - The effect of exchange rates on export activities has been identified by Sullivan and Bauerschmidt (1988). Their study found that European managers regarded a decline in the value of a currency relative to foreign markets as an important incentive underlying export activity. Other studies by Kenen and Rodrik (1986), Chowdury (1993) and Cushman (1988) examined the impact of exchange rate volatility on growth of foreign trade. It is concluded that the higher

the volatility of exchange rates, the higher the risk perceived by risk averse traders. Since the exchange rate is agreed on at the time of the trade contract, but the payment is often not made until future delivery takes place, it can create uncertainty about profits to be made and reduce the expected benefits of international trade (Hooper and Kohlhagen, 1978).

(ii) *Availability of finance* - Some findings reveal that lack of working capital to finance exports is one of the important barriers to firms' involvement in export activities (Tseng and Yu, 1991; Keng and Jiuan, 1989). Government policy that supports the availability and access of finance to businesses can consequently help in inducing exports.

(iii) *Inflation* - The effect of inflation on export activity is identified by Jeannet and Hennessey (1998) and Cateora and Graham (1999). The findings show that if a significant share of the production inputs is domestic, export industries in an inflationary economy must anticipate the situation where production costs are increasing at a faster rate than the sales price which is primarily governed by the world market.

(iv) *Taxes* - Tax is one of the most common incentives provided by government to promote exporting. Reduced tax rates on export income or duty drawback schemes on imports used to generate export sales are some examples of the tax schemes that can encourage both non-exporting and exporting firms to initiate or expand exporting activities.

3) Export assistance program – Export assistance programs are usually provided by government departments, trade associations, chambers of commerce, and embassies as well as trade missions. Kotabe and Czinkota (1992) classify export assistance into two types: export service programs and market development programs. Export service programs include seminars for potential exporters,

export counselling, how-to-export handbooks, and export financing. Market development programs, as stated by Lesch et al. (1990), include dissemination of sales leads to local firms, participation in trade shows, preparation of market analysis, and export newsletters. The fundamental thrust of export assistance, according to Gencturk and Kotabe (2001), is to reduce uncertainty in the process of decision making.

The most important issue examined in the empirical investigation of export assistance is the fit between the assistance needs and the assistance programs available. A study by Walters (1983) shows that there is a considerable gap between the actual needs of the firms and the services provided by the US Department of Commerce. In terms of the usage level, the study reveals that firms only use a few types of assistance for business activities and decision making processes. This followed from the fact that the information provided was not specifically meeting the needs of the companies. Other studies by Bradshaw et al. (2002), Crick and Chaudry (1997b), Young et al. (1999), Crick and Czinkota (1995), and Kedia and Chhokar (1986) also reveal a very similar conclusion. Diamantopoulos et al. (1993) found that the adoption of export promotion services requires an awareness of their availability. The preference to use the assistance also depends on the perceived usefulness of the program (Crick and Chaudry, 2000; Silverman et al., 2002). The alternative to this gap is, instead of providing firms with standardized information, to customize the information based on the specific needs of individual firms (Seringhaus, 1987).

In conjunction with the domestic external factors, there are factors in the export markets that have to be anticipated by the firms. Favourable foreign market conditions are just as important as the domestic market environment. The perception of too many problems in the export markets may also prevent firms from exporting. The most common factors found in the foreign market environment include level of competition, tariff barriers to trade, non-tariff barriers, and physical and psychological distance.

Level of competition – Level of competition in the foreign market was found to be the strongest barrier preventing the engagement of non-exporters in export activities (Leonidou, 1995b). It is also a major concern for firms who have been involved in exports for some times (Da Silva and Da Rocha, 2008; Dichtl et al., 1990; Kaynak and Kothari, 1984). Madsen (1989) found that foreign markets with little competition and high growth provide more favourable market conditions and thus contribute to export success.

Tariff barriers – Tariffs or taxes on imports of commodities into a country or region are found to be the most common type of trade control (Bradley, 1995). The common purpose of imposing tariffs is to provide revenue for the government and to protect domestic firms from foreign competitors. Anderson (2005) argues that tariffs that are set excessively high can block all trade and operate just like import bans. Bilateral trade agreements as well as regional trading blocks can help to reduce the impact of tariffs on trade as they are established mostly to diminish trade barriers between member countries

Non-tariff barriers – Non-tariff barriers have been found to be major inhibitors to exporting firms (see for example, Marouane et al., 2003; Bagchi-Sen, 1999). Non-tariff barriers are government measures other than tariffs that restrict imports.

Janzen and Frost from Western Centre for Economic Research (2000) define non-tariff barriers as including "invisible" trade barriers such as procedural delays, excessive documentation requirements, and lack of transparency and predictability in the application of government rules and regulations. According to Bourke and Leitch (1998), non-tariff barriers are even more difficult to evaluate than the tariff ones as their existence may serve other purposes beyond the trade restriction purpose.

Physical and psychological distance – Apart from the business opportunities provided by foreign markets, they also bring about challenges in routine operation. Differences in language, consumer behaviour, cultural standards, and/or legal framework pose separate pressures in addition to the purely physical issues (Bradley, 1995; Stottinger and Schleglemilch, 1998). The research findings show that the relation between cultural proximity and foreignness can be mapped by the construct of psychic distance (see for example Jain, 1989; Klein and Roth, 1990; O'Grady and Lane, 1996). Psychic distance, or a firm's degree of uncertainty about a foreign market resulting from cultural differences and other business difficulties that inhibit learning about the market and its operation, is often measured by using level of similarity/difference in a number of aspects. The comparison factors include language of the country, acceptance of business practices, economic environment, legal system and communication infrastructure

(Klein and Roth, 1990). Other studies emphasize the cultural aspect when measuring the psychic distance (see for example Ronen and Shenkar, 1985; Kogut and Singh, 1988; Benito and Gripsurd, 1992).

Based on Bradley's study (1995), it is concluded that companies tend to be more knowledgeable and have more information about foreign markets which are culturally near to them, than for more distant markets. This finding confirms the previous studies, that exporting tends to begin with the psychologically closest country, and then expand to psychologically more distant countries (Johanson and Wiedersheim-Paul, 1975). The increasing integration and interaction of world markets, however, has somewhat weakened the concept of psychic distance as the global market is considered to be increasingly homogeneous (Stottinger and Schlegelmilch, 1998).

2.5.3 The Internationalisation Stages: Export Development of a Firm

Most companies usually choose export operation as an initial mode of entry into international markets (Albaum et al., 1998). There are evidences that firms only gradually develop their business in international markets (Boter and Holmquist, 1996). The concept of the export development process, that is part of the internationalisation process of a firm, has not been uniformly defined by authors (Johansen and Vahlne, 1977; Welch and Luostarinen, 1988). From the viewpoint of SMEs, the internationalisation process can be seen as an evolutionary process of development in their international engagement (Rialp and Rialp, 2001). In this sequential process, a firm gathers foreign experience and accumulates organisational learning over time. The increase in the firm's level of international involvement will also lead to a change in their methods of serving foreign markets. The greater the international involvement a firm has, the deeper and more diverse its offering to foreign markets will be.

Several models have been applied to conceptualize the process of export development. The majority of these models highlight the process as a series of incremental decisions, rather than large, dramatic foreign investments. Firms are believed to move through stages as their commitment to foreign markets increases. This section provides a review of the existing staged models and their relevance in explaining how the individual firm is engaged in export activities.

According to Gankema et al. (2000) and Chetty and Campbell-Hunt (2004), there are two major approaches dominating the incremental internationalisation perspective: the Uppsala internationalisation model (U-model) and Innovation-related models (I-models). Although one model was developed in Sweden and the other in the USA, they both share the same concept that firms engage in international activities in incremental steps and through distinct stages (Hammoudi, 2005).

The U-model or the Uppsala model was introduced by Johanson and Wiedersheim-Paul (1975). The model is based on the study of four major Swedish firms – Sandvik, Atlas Copco, Facit and Volvo. The conclusions drawn from this study, show that the successive stages represent higher degrees of international involvement and therefore a greater commitment of resources to overseas markets. In this model, Johanson and Wiedersheim-Paul chose to distinguish between four different stages, with regard to the degree of involvement of the firm in international operations. The stages in this model are:

1) No regular export activities

2) Export to psychologically close countries via independent representation (agent);

3) Exporting to psychologically distant countries/establishment of an overseas sales subsidiary;

4) Overseas production/manufacturing units are established in the foreign country.

In this study, the most important obstacles to internationalisation are lack of knowledge and resources. These obstacles are reduced through incremental decision making and learning about the foreign market and operations. Then, as the perceived risk of market investment decreases, the internationalisation process is furthered by the increased need to control sales, by exposure to offers and demands, and to extend overseas operations (Johanson and Wiedersheim-Paul, 1975). According to Leonidou and Katsikeas (1996) the model emphasizes the critical role of information acquisition in every stage of internationalisation. Knowledge acquired leads to reduced levels of uncertainty regarding foreign markets and operation.

In 1977, Bilkey and Tesar (1977) developed a stage hierarchy approach based on Roger's theory of diffusion of innovations, known as the I-model. The study took its data from a sample of small and medium-sized firms in Wisconsin, USA. The analytical methodology used requires treating each stage of the export development process as the dependent variable in a multiple regression equation; coefficients differing at each stage allowed for experience gained in preceding stages (Thomas & Araujo, 1985). The results of the study mainly conclude that: 1) The export development process of firms tends to proceed in stages; 2) Considerations that influence a firm's progression from one stage to another tend to differ by stage; 3) Within the size range of firms studied, size was relatively unimportant when account was taken of the quality and dynamism of management.

The Bilkey and Tesar (1977) study divided the process into a six-staged model that consists of:

1) Management is not interested in exporting and will not even fill unsolicited orders.
2) Management is willing to fill unsolicited orders, but makes no effort to explore the feasibility of actively exporting.
3) Management actively explores the feasibility of exporting (this stage may be omitted if a firm receives unsolicited orders).
4) The firm exports experimentally to one or a few psychologically close countries.
5) The firm is an experienced exporter to the country/ies it exports to and will make optimal export adjustments based on changes in environmental factors.
6) Management explores the feasibility of exporting to additional markets that are psychologically further away.

In 1982, Cavusgil proposed a model consisting of four stages. The criteria used in distinguishing firms in various stages include: management level of awareness of foreign opportunities;, the nature of search processes for information; decision-making mode of management; typical decision-making skills utilised; and the nature of international marketing involvement. The stages proposed are as follows:

1) Non-exporting firms. Not interested in gathering export-related information.

2) Non-exporting firms. Interested in gathering export related information. (These two stages may be grouped as the "pre-involvement stage").

3) Exporting firms. Export less than 10 per cent of their output. (Referred to as the limited/experimental involvement stage).

4) Exporting firms. Exports more than 10 per cent of their output (Referred to as the active involvement stage).

The study's findings primarily conclude that: 1) During the pre-involvement stage, non-exporting firms are not interested in gathering export related information. 2) New product development capability and product quality are the main impetus of the progression from stage one to stage two. 3) Second stage firms were found to be more active in gathering export related information than stage-one firms. 4) Managers in stage-two firms are more likely to be younger and more educated than those of stage-one firms. 5) Stage-three firms are more likely to enjoy management expertise in marketing and finance than those of stage-two firms. 6) Progression to stage four is facilitated more by the presence of a technologically intensive product.

Wortzel and Wortzel (1981) developed a five-stage model based on their study in five Asian countries: three newly industries countries and two least developed countries. The five stages were based on marketing mix elements and the degree of control exerted by the exporter in overseas operations. The stages were as follows:

1) Importer pull – At this stage the firm has not made an explicit decision to seek exports, their export business is initiated by an importer who therefore dominates in various operations such as appearance, packaging,

shipping, and quality control. The local producer is simply a seller of production capacity.

2) Basic production, capacity marketing – At this stage there is some commitment to exporting and "exporter push" has started. Some internal design skills are developed, but the firm's most powerful weapon is low prices. The firm is still a seller of production capacity rather than product.

3) Advanced production, capacity marketing – At this stage the products satisfy consumer expectations. The firm begins to be more dominant in gaining control over the elements of marketing mix. Its marketing organisation becomes more skilled. A firm in this stage is a supplier of know how as well as of production capacity. However, price is still its major competitive weapon.

4) Product marketing, channel push – At this stage the firm produces for its own inventory rather than for customers only. The firm's investments and operations are considerably higher than that of firms in stage 3. With regard to the product, the firm is more dominant than its importer, and the responsibility in designing the product belongs to the firm. The firm may perform some marketing functions such as promotion. The firm has access to the technology levels of its competitors so that the limitations are more to do with marketing than production. Price is still an important competitive advantage.

5) Product marketing, consumer pull – This is the stage the marketing efforts shift from "channel push" to "consumer pull". The firm differentiates its offerings either through branding or distinctive fashion and style. The price is no longer the most important factor but product features. The firm in this stage will be actively engaged in trade promotion, in advertising to consumers, and in product design.

The findings of this study conclude that: 1) Stage 5 was theoretical in the newly industrialized and less developed countries where the study was carried out. 2) There are four main factors that help to determine the stage in which particular exporters are found. They are firms' experiences with the product; product marketing requirements; structure of distribution; and the existence of trade barriers imposed either by actions of market participants or by regulations.

Following the development of the above stage models, several researchers have also attempted to develop their own staged models. A brief review of those models is as follows: 1) A study by Reid (1981) has further developed the Bilkey and Tesar model. Based on the findings of the study, it is concluded that "decision maker's attitudes towards and preferences for foreign markets and export entry, together with his perception and expectations of the results from such entry, are major determinants of the subsequent export behaviour" (Reid, 1981:110); 2) A study by Czinkota (1982) has generated a six-stage model consisting of a completely uninterested firm; partially interested firm; experimental exporter; experienced small exporter and final stage, experienced large exporter; 3) A study by Moon and Lee (1990) develops a three-stage model. The stages proposed are lower, middle, and higher stages; 4) A four-stage model was developed by Lim et al. (1991). The model consists of awareness, interest, intention, and adoption stages; 5) Rao and Naidu (1992) offer a four-stage model consisting of non-exporters, export intenders, sporadic exporters, and regular exporters.

In their review of empirical models, Leonidou and Katsikeas (1996) suggested that despite differences among the various models as to number, nature, and content of the stages, the export development process can be divided into three broad phases of pre-engagement, initial and advanced stages. The review concluded that the pre-engagement phase includes three types of firms: those selling their goods in the domestic market and not interested in exporting; those involved in the domestic marker but seriously considering exporting; and those that used to export in the past but no longer do so. Firms in the initial phase were defined as those involved in sporadic export activity. In this phase, companies were classified as those having the potential to increase their overseas involvement, and those unable to cope with the demands of exporting, leading to marginal export behaviour or withdrawal from selling abroad altogether. Firms in the advanced phase were classified as regular exporters with extensive overseas experience and frequently consider more committed forms of international business.

Apart from the general acknowledgment of these stage models in the existing literature, many other studies have cast doubt on and criticized them. Some authors such as Diamantopoulos and Inglis (1988), Sullivan and Bauerschmidt (1990), argued that the underlying assumption that firms develop through stages in their internationalisation process is far from universal in time and sequence. This can be observed in the description of the models and the variability in the number of stages, commonly ranging from three to as many as six. Andersen (1993) also noted that the stage models lack explanatory power as to how the process takes place or how movements between stages can be predicted. The boundaries between stages are claimed to be not clearly defined, leading to confusion as to when a specific stage begins and ends.

It is also claimed that most models do not readily accommodate the reality of reversals in the direction of change and sufficiently take into consideration the transition phases from one stage to another; Some firms may even omit some of the stages making the adoption process much quicker (Cannon and Willis, 1981). Other researchers argue that some firms are international at their inception (see for example Harveston et al., 2000; Moen, 2002; Oviatt and McDougall, 1994), indicating that internationalisation patterns and purposes of individual firms are quite unique and highly situation specific (Reid, 1983). Significant progress in various aspects of technology as well as the shifting mind-set of international markets has been claimed to be the reason for the international at inception phenomenon (Harveston et al., 2000; Moen, 2002; Oviatt and McDougall, 1994). The variation in knowledge and experience of firm's top management is also maintained to be a critical resource that contributes to an early adoption of export and internationalisation (Reuber and Fischer, 1997). This reasoning indicates that firms may skip or compress stages in the export development process through well-planned engagement and commitment.

Due to the criticisms above, other researchers suggest an alternative "network" approach to export development models. The focus of this approach is on the relationships that develop amongst firms which help to increase their knowledge and other resources needed to successfully internationalize (Berry and Brock, 2004; Coviello and Munro, 1995, Coviello and Munro, 1997). An assumption used in the network model is that the firm's export development varies according to the resources controlled by other firm. A firm usually gains access to these external resources due to their network positions. Although the network approach of export development offers an important element of understanding key issues involved in cooperation in industrial systems and of global industry competition, this approach has drawn criticism for having limited strength in understanding the internationalisation pattern, and not offering very precise conclusions while including too many variables (Bjorkman and Forsgren, 2000). It is also criticized for not offering a satisfactory model for predictions (Bjorkman and Forsgren, 2000) and ignoring the way firms overcome the problems within their network relationship (Chetty and Blankenburg Hol, 2000). Thus, since the network model focuses mainly on larger firms and rarely explains how SMEs use networks in their internationalisation (Nummela, 2002), the model simply adds to the consensus that the whole internationalisation process is much more complex and less structured than was suggested by earlier theories and models.

2.6 The Conceptual Framework of the Determinants of Export Development of a Firm

The earlier sections have been devoted to reviewing a wide range of literature on determinants of export behaviour and the development of export in the firm. This section turns to a model development which attempted to conceptualize the relationship between managerial and organisational determinants of export behaviour and export development in the firm. The determinants of export behaviour are expected to vary along with the differences in a firm's level of export development.

Following the pioneering Uppsala model of Johansen and Vahlne (1977), a number of studies have concentrated almost exclusively on finding the relationship between market environmental/behavioural variables and foreign activities. Most of the studies, however, according to Cavusgil and Nevin (1981), lacked systematic empirical analysis. In 1978, Wiedersheim-Paul, Olson and Welch developed a model that stresses the role of a firm's "pre-export' activities in its export initiation. The model concentrates on three main factors namely the decision maker, the environment of the firm and firm itself. The model assumed that all firms are non-exporters in the beginning and sell to local markets and that there is only one decision maker in the firm who makes all important decisions.

Figure 2.1: Factors Affecting the Pre-export Activities of the Firm

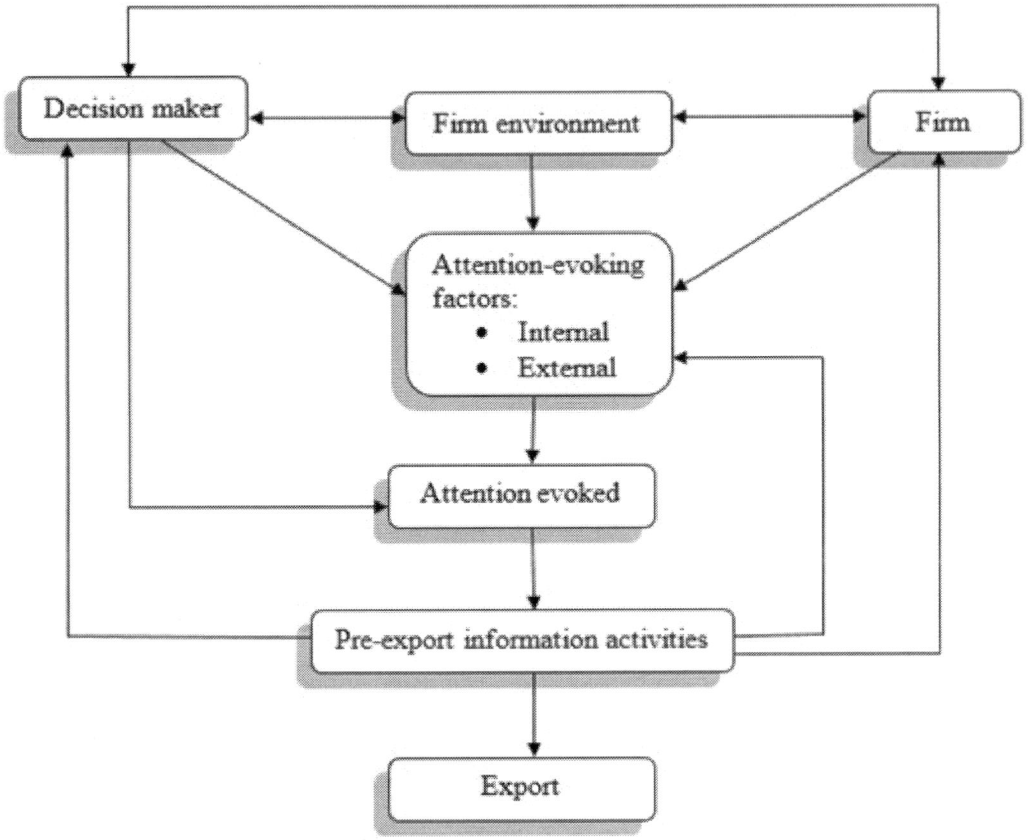

Decision maker

Firm environment

Firm

Attention-evoking factors:

- Internal
- External

Attention evoked

Pre-export information activities

Export

Source: Wiedersheim-Paul, Olson and Welch, 1978.

The decision maker in this model is subject to different kinds of attention evoking factors or those factors that can trigger a firm to consider exporting as a possible strategy. The type and amount of attention and how it is perceived by the decision maker is contingent upon the characteristics of the decision maker, the environment of the firm and the firm itself, as well as the interaction between these factors. The decision maker characteristics include such aspects as international outlook, degree of international orientation and perception of uncertainty. The environment of the firm was defined in relation to the location of the firm in the domestic market. Location is considered significant in reducing transportation costs and fostering information flows. Firm characteristics such as its goal and degree of realisation, type of product line, history of the firm, and degree of extra-regional expansion were considered influential in determining pre-export behaviour of a firm.

Attention-evoking factors in this model can be broadly classified into internal and external to the firm. Internal factors included such factors as differential firm advantage like the possession of unique competencies, and excess capacity in the resources of management, marketing, production, or finance. Under external-evoking factors, fortuitous orders from foreign customers, competition stimuli arising either from domestic or foreign competitors, market opportunities, and government export stimulation activities were identified.

In 1981, Cavusgil and Nevin proposed a model that emphasized a number of background and intervening variables (see Figure 3.2). Their model described export-marketing behaviour as a merging of two background variables namely differential firm advantages and managerial aspirations for business goals. Differential firm advantages are derived from the firm's products features, technological orientation and resources. The managerial aspirations variables underscore such dimensions as growth, profits, and market development. Cavusgil and Nevin's (1981) findings put the view that the reluctance of a firm to export is a consequence of the lack of determination of management and that management requires a long-range commitment in order to achieve success in export markets.

Figure 2.2: The Path Model of a Firms' Export Behaviour

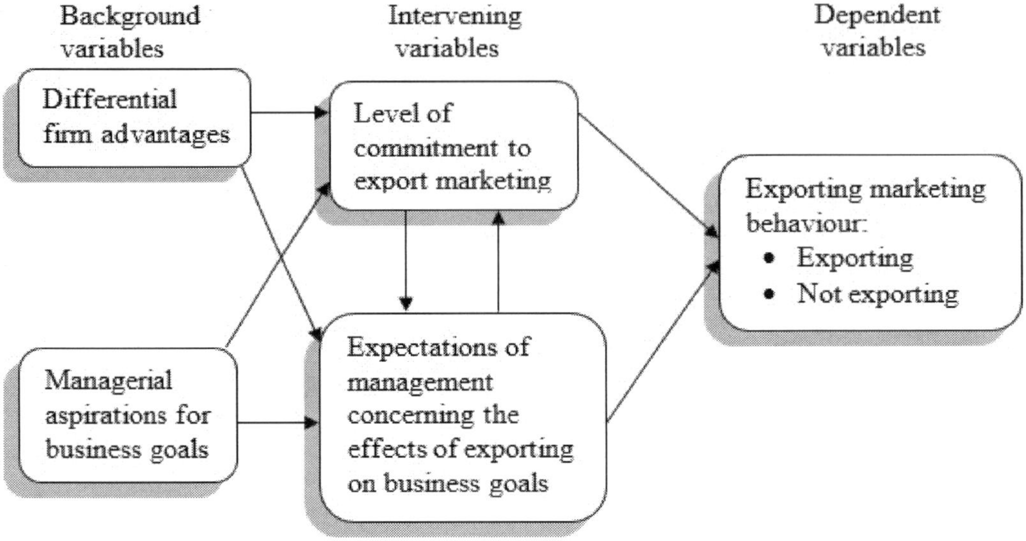

Background variables

Intervening variables

Dependent variables

Differential firm advantages

Level of commitment to export marketing

Exporting marketing behaviour:

- Exporting
- Not exporting

Managerial aspirations for business goals

Expectations of management concerning the effects of exporting on business goals

Source: Cavusgil and Nevin, 1981.

Ibeh and Young (2001) conceptualized the export entrepreneurial model from the perspective of Nigerian firms (see Figure 3.3). Their model was based on the notion that exporting is an 'entrepreneurial act'. The authors maintained that this concept of the entrepreneurial act is particularly useful in developing countries due to environmental problems and the increasing need for an entrepreneurial orientation which is often lacking in small sized and resource-deficient firms. They recommend strengthening firms' entrepreneurial foundations in order to improve export behaviour or performance. They also suggested some kind of assessment of entrepreneurial orientation in order to have better insights into the export potential of non-exporting firms.

Figure 2.3: The Export Entrepreneurial Model

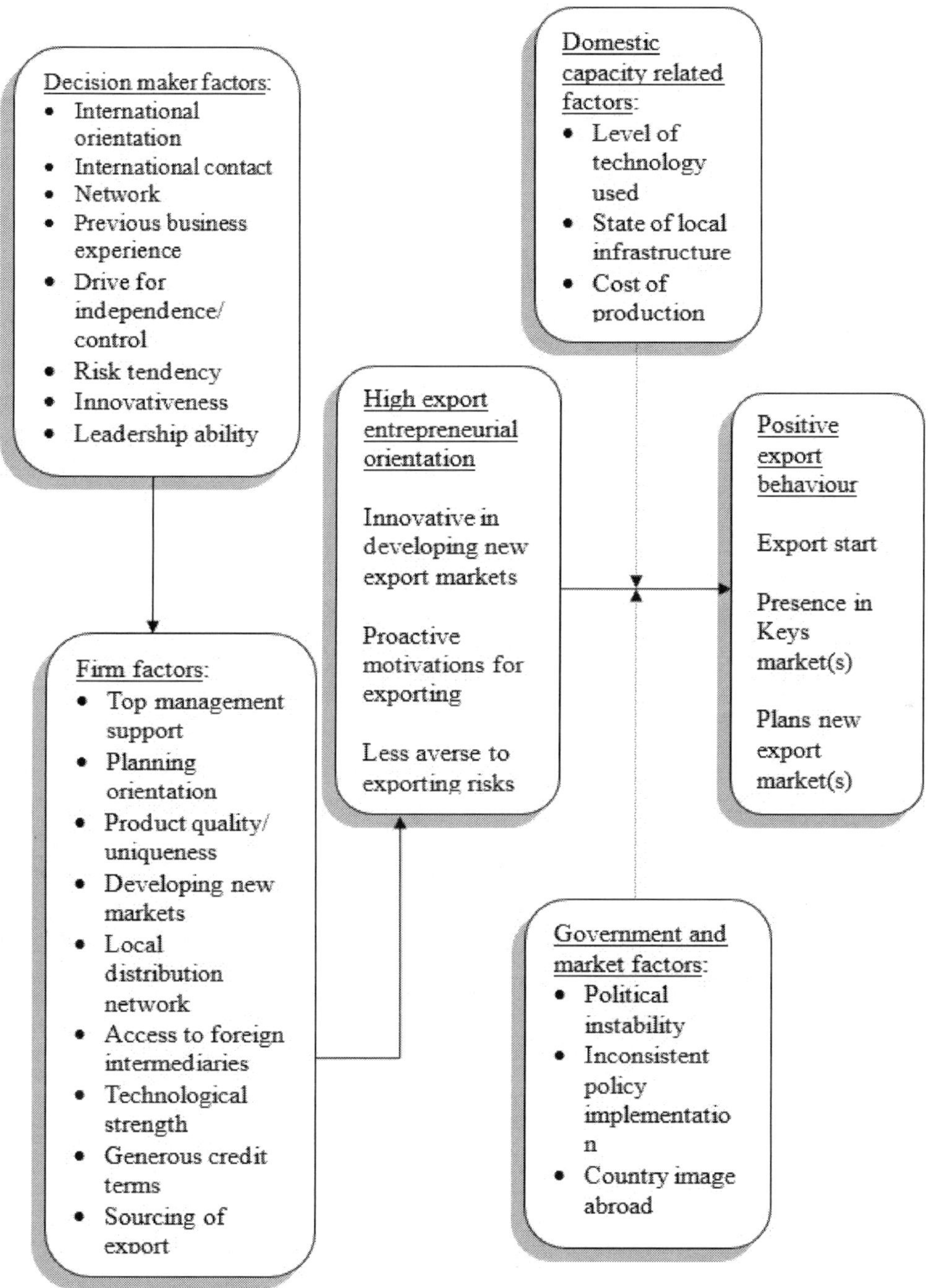

Source: Ibeh and Young, 2001.

In examining export development behaviour in the Spanish wine industry, Suarez-Ortega and Alamo-Vera proposed a model with three distinct categories of resources and capabilities that influence export behaviour: 1) firm specific resources and capabilities; 2) management characteristics; and 3) management attitude and perceptions (see Figure 3.4). All dimensions, except size, under these three broad categories influence non-exporters and exporters in the export development proxies of export intention, export propensity, and export intensity.

Figure 2.4: Internal Determinants of Export Involvement

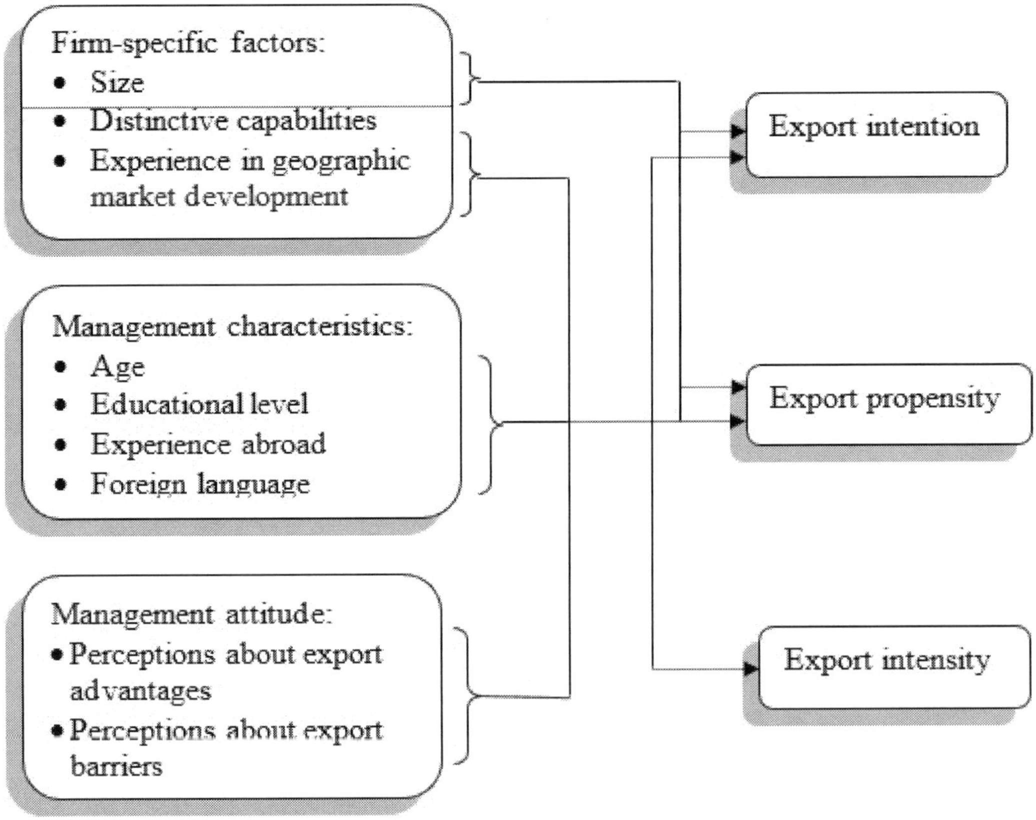

Source: Suarez-Ortega and Alamo-Vera, 2005.

The model suggests that the main driving forces motivating internationalisation are found within the firm, and therefore they are based on management's strengths and weaknesses. Rather than the external environment, the pool of resources and capabilities within the firm that might be appropriately combined is the main influence on the internationalisation endeavour. The authors further recommend assistance programs aimed at enhancing managers' skills and capabilities in order to accelerate and support the internationalisation process. Export promotion programs should emphasize activities that increase managers' awareness of export advantage in order to get more non-exporters interested in exporting.

2.7 Chapter Summary

The review of literature in this chapter has concluded that there were at least four theoretical bases at the macro level as the grounds for this research. Most of the theories attempted to provide economic reasons for international trade, international trade patterns, and product-market evolution. Within this macro understanding of trade, it is obvious that there are potential benefits that can be gained from exporting. None of these theories alone, however, can explain all aspects of trade flows between countries.

In the micro considerations, there are a number of possible taxonomies to distinguish the degree of a firm's export development. This micro approach is selected on the grounds that the macro approaches were inadequate in describing the export behaviour of the individual business unit where managerial and organisational characteristics of each individual firm greatly impact on export behaviour. The decision to get involved in export activities and the likelihood of succeeding in export markets have been found to be strongly related to management's positive perceptions as well as distinct managerial and organisational background characteristics.

In addition to the internal characteristics of the firm, export behaviour models have also studied the impact of external determinants on a firm's involvement in exporting. There are two major classifications covered under external determinants, they are domestic external determinants and the foreign external determinants. Under the domestic external determinants, there are size and state of the domestic market and export promotion program; while foreign external determinants include level of competition, tariff and non-tariff barriers, and physical and psychological distance. It is generally noted that favourable external conditions are more preferred by firms than adverse external conditions as the latter can inhibit a firm's progression along the internationalisation path. Although it is pivotal to consider the external determinants in the analysis, the complexity and dynamism of these factors have constrained this current research to focus on factors internal to the firm. External factors will be incorporated as part of managerial perception variables which represent external barriers to export development.

The final part of this chapter has reviewed a number of conceptual frameworks explaining the relationship between managerial and organisational determinants of export behaviour and export development in the firm. Despite differences among the models regarding the determinants of export behaviour, it can be concluded that different sets of organisational and managerial determinants influence the different stages of the export development process and these dimensions are expected to recur over time due to the common characteristics of this internationalized mode of entry.

****

CHAPTER THREE

METHODOLOGICAL FRAMEWORK

3.1 Introduction

The literature review in Chapters 2 highlighted a number of preconditions to support the need to examine manufacturing SMEs' behaviour in Indonesia. Some important findings showed that most of the government policies to promote SME development in Indonesia were evidently not effective due to the lack of a systematic plan and government capabilities (World Bank in Wie, 2006). Further studies of Indonesian manufacturing SMEs' export behaviour were inadequate to the extent where it is deemed necessary to develop an empirical model to help understand and confirm critical variables affecting SMEs development in overseas markets (Leonidou, 1995).

This chapter serves as the methodological chapter where the specification of managerial and organisational factors related to the firm's export development are conceptualized and operationalized. The structure of this chapter is as follows. Section 3.2 describes the critical linkage between the model specification of all predictors and export development. Section 3.3 elaborates the manner in which each variable is made operational within the model. Data source descriptions and collection methods are discussed in Section 3.4. The major statistical techniques used in the data analysis are presented in Section 3.5. The chapter draws its conclusion in Section 3.6.

3.2 Organisational and Managerial Characteristics and Export Development - the Critical Linkages

The literature review discussed in Chapter 2 illustrates the need for an overview in a developing county context such as Indonesia. The most recent review of empirical studies (Suarez-Ortega and Alamo-Vera, 2005) revealed an absence of export behaviour studies carried out in developing countries. Furthermore, most studies focus on the managerial characteristics and direct effects of exporting without trying to construct a framework that investigates the relationships and interactions between the variables. Therefore, there is a need for a new approach that incorporates the most common factors of firm and managerial characteristics, including managerial perceptions, and that explores and understands their relationship and interaction in different stages of the export development process.

Building upon the review discussed, this current study uses five categories to distinguish between the various determinants of export behaviour: managerial characteristics; organisational characteristics; export development; export propensity; and export intensity. All managerial perceptions about internal and external export barriers, export benefits, and firm distinctive capabilities are included under managerial characteristics and are considered as predictor variables. Since Indonesia has been pursuing an incremental approach in its economic development policy by initially focusing on import substitution, most Indonesian SMEs are assumed to have been following a gradualist approach to entering foreign markets. For measurement purposes, the study follows the generic export development stages of Leonidou and Katsikeas' (1996) study. That study also used proxies of export propensity and export intention to support the export development classification.

Figure 3.1: Organisational and Managerial determinants of Export Development

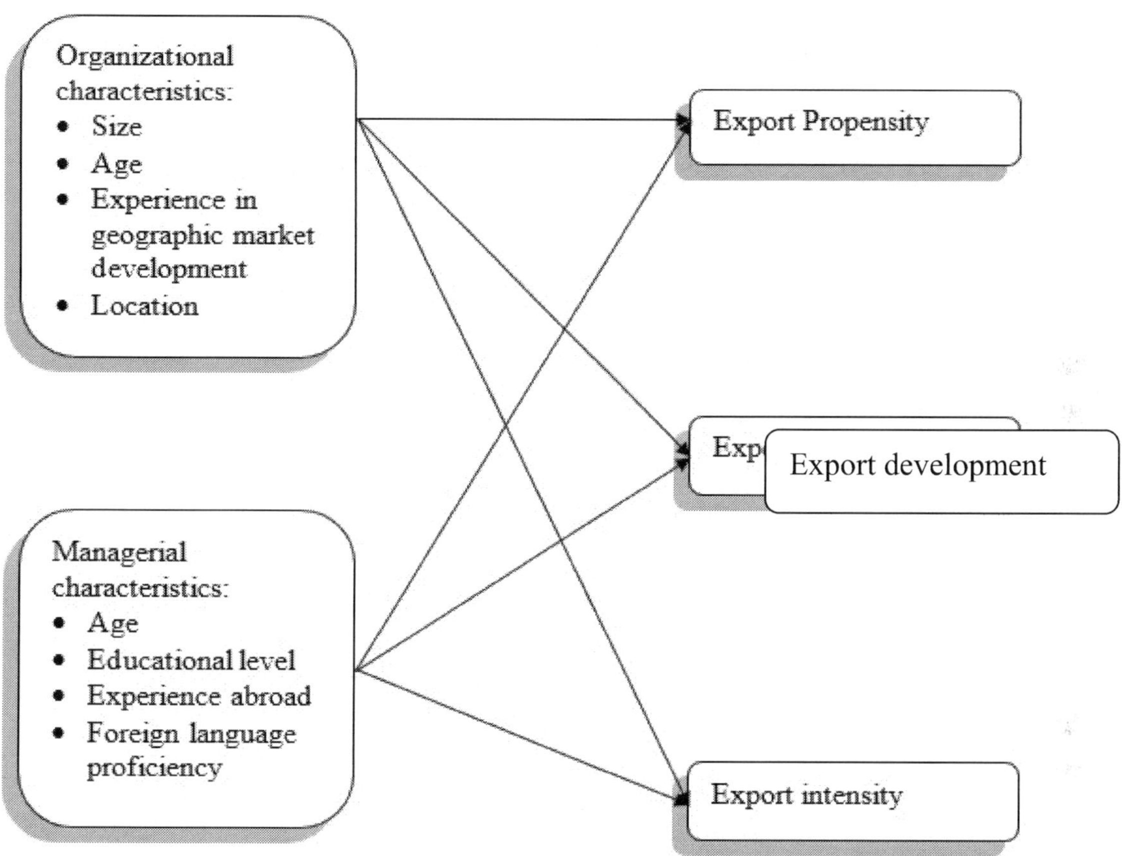

The proposed conceptual framework of this study, as depicted in Figure 3.1, shows all predictors belonging to the internal environment of the firm listed under 'firm characteristics' and 'managerial characteristics'. All perception variables that stem from managerial aptitude assessment are classified in managerial characteristics. The correlation between each organisational specific resource and management background characteristic will determine the firm's level of export development, export propensity, and export intensity. Despite their significance as barriers to exporting, the external/uncontrollable factors have received the least research attention (Gripsurd, 1990) but in this study, they are included as components in managerial perceived export barriers. To sum up, the concepts used to develop the proposed conceptual framework resemble Suarez-Ortega and Alamo-Vera's (2005) research closely, but improve on the older technique by using factor analysis and structural equation approaches to solve the multidimensional correlations and relationships between each variable in the model.

3.3 Operationalisation of Variables and Research Hypothesis

3.3.1 Independent Variables - Managerial Determinants

Before turning to specific variables note, for measurement purposes, this study is following Dichtl et al. (1983) objective-subjective typology of management characteristics (Dichtl et al. 1983, 1984, 1990; Leonidou et al.; 1998, Suarez-Ortega and Alamo-Vera, 2005) and will analyse those managerial influences under these two main groups as shown in Table 3.1.

Table 3.1: Subjective-Objective Typology of Management Characteristics

	Subjective Characteristics	Objective Characteristics
1.	Risk aversion	Age
2.	Change aversion	Educational level
3.	Personal ambition	Language proficiency
4.	Innovation	Experience abroad
5.	Dynamism	
6.	Flexibility	

It is stated that objective managerial characteristics can explain more variance in the organisational behaviour than the underlying psychological constructs. Wiersema and Bantel (1992), for example, claimed that some demographic characteristics help explain firms' strategic behaviour as they are a manifestation of managerial psychological dimensions. The emphasis on demographic characteristics rather than the psychological nature of management was also justified by Hambrick and Mason (1984) and Albaum et al. (1998) who argued that some of the background characteristics do not provide measurable physical entities and are therefore more difficult to measure than objective managerial characteristics. This study will adopt the objective managerial typology which influences firms' export development processes and each characteristic will be made operational as follows:

3.3.1.1 Age of the Manager

In an attempt to explain the export behavior of SMEs, many empirical studies have included the age of the entrepreneur as a determinant in their analysis. Wroon and Pahl (1971), for example, have found that the average age of the top management team has been negatively associated with high-risk decision making. It was also found by Taylor (1975) that age is negatively associated with the ability to analyse new information. A positive link between age and export behaviour was highlighted by the Atabay (2008), Westhead et al. (2002), and Suarez-Ortega and Alamo Vera (2005) studies which suggested that the older the managers the more export oriented they are than their younger counterparts. Other scholars such as Oviatt et al. (1993) and Moon and Lee (1990) argue that younger managers are more open to extending their company's activities in foreign markets as compared to older managers. Younger managers, in addition, are claimed to be more internationally minded and cosmopolitan that older ones (Moon and Lee, 1990). Despite these conflicting findings, a notion on which there is some consensus is that younger managers, due to their age, tend to be more open to challenges and risks. Hence, they would be likely to take advantage of any export possibilities and show greater attempts to expand their operation abroad than their older counterparts (Oviatt et al, 1993 and Ursic and Czinkota, 1989). Then, it would be reasonable to hypothesize that:

H1: Manager's age has a negative effect on the level of export development, thus having a negative effect on export propensity and intensity.

The manager's age is made operational, based on Suarez-Ortega and Alamo-Vera's (1985) findings, by gathering data from respondents in the five age group options provided.

3.3.1.2 Educational Level

Several empirical studies have supported the view that knowledge and skills attained through the entrepreneur's own life or education, that are then utilized in firms, can become a key determinant of the firm's long-term success. That is, the higher the level of education that mangers have, the more likely they are to be objective in evaluating the benefits and technical know-how of exporting (Garnier, 1982, Samiee and Walters, 1999) and to possess more managerial knowledge and capabilities (Burton and Schlegelmilch, 1987) that can be applied to improve export productivity and performance. The positive link between the educational level of the manager and the degree of export involvement is highlighted by Axinn (1988) and Oviatt et al. (1993). Suarez-Ortega and Alamo-Vera (2005) and Manolova et al. (2002), however, found manager's education to have no significant influence on export development. Despite these conflicting results, better educated decision makers are expected to have better problem solving ability, discipline, motivation and self confidence to enter foreign markets (Oviatt et al. 1993). Therefore, this study hypothesizes that:

H2: Manager's educational level has a positive effect on the level of export development, thus having a positive effect on export propensity and intensity.

The manager's educational level is made operational, based on Suarez-Ortega and Alamo-Vera's (2005) study, by the inclusion of a variable that collects educational level in four options: no education; primary/secondary education; undergraduate; and postgraduate.

3.3.1.3 Experience Abroad

Experience abroad refers to the manager's exposure to the foreign cultures and business practices during the time spent abroad while studying, working, or travelling on business interest or tourism. Leonidou et al. (1998) noted that the time managers have spent abroad is an important factor which could explain export intention, propensity, and intensity, because it involves managers' exposure to foreign cultures, which allows for an accumulation of greater experiential knowledge about international markets. Barrett and Wilkinson (1986) and Reuber and Fischer (1997) studies confirmed that internationally experienced management has a greater propensity to demonstrate positive behaviours associated with a higher degree of internationalisation than those managers without any international experience. Furthermore, Da Rocha et al. (1990) found that managers who travelled abroad are more exposed to foreign business practices, meet future customers, and spot market opportunities than those who are not. Based on these findings, this study proposes that:

H3: Manager's experience abroad has a positive effect on the level of export development, thus having a positive effect on export propensity and intensity.

The operation of managerial experience abroad is based on Mpinganjira's (2004) study; the respondents have to indicate their previous experience abroad from five options:

- I was born overseas.
- My parents were born abroad.

- I was born into a business family.
- I have lived/worked abroad for sometime
- I received some/all of my education abroad

3.3.1.4 Foreign Language Proficiency

Dichtl et al. (1990), Davis (1995), and Leonidou et al. (1998) conclude that language proficiency is positively associated with export development since this skill may help to establish social and business contacts abroad, improve communication and interaction with foreign customers, assist in understanding foreign business practices, and facilitate effective planning and control in overseas markets. This, in turn, increases the proximity between the manager and the foreign country context. Turnbull and Welhalm (1985) support this notion by maintaining that the lack of foreign language knowledge may increase the manager's perception of psychological distance between the domestic market and the international one, and therefore, negatively affect the export behaviour of the firm. Furthermore, Obben and Magagula's (2003) recent study of Swaziland's SMEs highlighted the significant importance of foreign language proficiency on firms' propensity for export operations, particularly in the context of developing countries. Thus, it is logical to hypothesise that:

H4: Manager's foreign language proficiency has a positive effect on the level of export development, thus having a positive effect on export propensity and intensity.

To parameterize manager's foreign language proficiency, the respondents have rehash to indicate foreign language(s) and their proficiency level in the language(s).

3.3.2 Independent Variables - Organisational Determinants

3.3.2.1 Firm Size

Size is one of the variables most frequently referred to in the export development process (Reid, 1982). Size as an indicator of organisational resource capability (Pedersen and Petersen, 1998) is expected to have a positive effect on exporting. The internationalisation process, which often requires an increasing demand in resources, was strongly correlated with size (Cavusgil, 1984; Johanson and Vahlne, 1977; Johanson and Wiedersheim-Paul, 1975). It is assumed that the larger the firm, the greater the firm's ability to expand resources and absorb risks. Such firms may also have a higher bargaining power (Erramilli and Rao, 1993). The larger firms are the more likely they are to become international. Size, however, as suggested by Bonnacorsi (1992), should not be directly associated with export intensity (export sales/total sales) because once the firm is engaged in exporting, the ratio of export sales to total sales can result from a change in either the numerator (that is, export sales) or denominator (that is, total sales) or both. Moreover, several studies (Bonaccorsi, 1992; Alonso and Donoso in Suarez-Ortega, 2005) have shown no association or, in fact, a negative relationship between size and export intensity. Based on the above discussion, this study proposes the following hypothesis:

H5: Firm's size has a positive effect on export development and export propensity, but a negative effect on export intensity.

Several indicators have been used in the literature to measure firm size and it seems that the number of full-time employees and sales volume are the most popular. Other studies have included total assets, equity and deposits, and domestic market sales (Agarwal and Ramaswami, 1992). In the context of this study, the total number of full-time employees and assets value (excluding land and building) were selected as indicators of firm size due to consensus and compliance reasons. This selection was also based on previous studies that indicated managers would be more willing to provide employment and asset range information in comparison with alternative size criteria such as sales volume (Katsikeas and Morgan, 1994). Furthermore as argued by these authors, employment figures are considered to be more predictable because they are not influenced by price fluctuations. Assets value is also selected not only to validate the employment figures but also to justify the argument that small firms may be more productive than large ones due to a higher capital-labour ratio. Drawing on the above discussion, this study will differentiate firm size based on the number of full time employees and will consider the following three firm sizes:

1. Small firms, with employment of between 5 and 19 workers
2. Medium-sized firms, with employment of 20 and 300 workers.
3. Large firms, with more than 300 workers.

The size of firms will also be classified based on the amount of assets (excluding land and building) owned. The classification uses that developed by the Indonesian Central Bank (2004) to classify firms sizes.

1. Small firms, with total assets of Rp 200 million or less (excluding land and building).
2. Medium-sized firms, with total assets between Rp 200 million and Rp 10 billion (excluding land and building).

3. Large firms, with total assets of more than Rp 10 billion (excluding land and building).

3.3.2.2 Firm's Age

Most studies measure firm age as the number of years a firm has been in operation. Firm age can explain the extent of accumulated knowledge from which a firm can build its capabilities and provide it with better leverage to compete in international markets (Graner and Isaksson, 2002, van Dijk, 2002).

A positive significant relationship between firm age and exports is hypothesized based on the idea that the internationalisation of firms follows a step-wise learning process and since age is considered an accumulation of knowledge and experience, the established firms are more likely to export than the inexperienced ones. A number of studies such as Bilkey and Tesar (1977), Johanson and Vahlne (1977), Majocchi et al. (2005) and Welch and Wiedersheim-Paul (1980) found a positive effect of firm age and export behaviour. Most of the research, however, disclosed a negative relationship (see for example: Aggrey et al. 2010; Clarke, 2005; Fryges, 2006; Wengel and Rodriguez, 2006). These studies found that, 2005 younger firms are more interested in foreign operations than older ones. A firm younger by one year, in particular, was highlighted to have an export ratio higher than its five-year-old counterpart (see Wengel and Rodriguez, 2006). This could be because younger firms tend to perceive export as the only way to increase sales and achieve growth as opposed to the older firms which are often well-established in the domestic market. Other studies that have found no correlation between firm's age and export involvement are those by Bell (1995) and Keng and Jiuan (1989). Based on this discussion as well as Wengel and Rodriguez's (2006) findings in the Indonesian context, this study proposed the following hypothesis:

H6: Firm's age has a positiven effect on the level of export development, thus having a positive effect on export propensity and intensity.

3.3.2.3 Firm's Experience in Geographic Market Development

Previous studies found that the firm's export initiation was highly associated with its growth in the domestic market (Suarez-Ortega and Alamo-Vera, 2005; Beamish et al., 1993; Cavusgil, 1984; Cavusgil and Nevin, 1981). This is generally based on the assumptions made by the Uppsala internationalisation model which contends that the firm will grow within its domestic market before developing foreign markets (Johanson and Wiedersheim-Paul, 1975). In addition, it is stated that as soon as a firm expands its operations into more distant regions within its domestic market, it is moving into less familiar territory with more problems and costs of communication (Wiedersheim Paul et al. 1978). The relative foreignness of these distant markets is reduced as these barriers are overcome. During the process of this familiarisation phase, the firm is likely to develop skills in marketing a product at a distance, and extend its communications network. The limitations of the domestic market motivate firms to find an alternative through foreign market opportunities (Reid, 1983), thus facilitating the accomplishment of a higher export commitment. Based on this knowledge and sequential nature of the internationalisation process, this study hypothesizes that:

H7: Firm's geographic market development has a positive effect on the level of export development, thus having a positive effect on export propensity and intensity.

The parameter for a firm's experience in the geographic market is based on Axinn's (1985) research whereby the respondents have to indicate the current market area that best describes the geographic scope of the firm's products from a five point option: local; provincial; regional; more than one region of a nation; and nation wide.

3.3.2.4 Firm's Location

Firm's location in the context of this study represents the place where the office or manufacturing plants are located, which can influence the firm's export intention, propensity and/or intensity. Based on Wiedersheim-Paul et al. (1978), it is assumed that the geographic proximity of firms to transportation centres, facilitates the export development of firms due to cost effectiveness. Given that the degree of economic and infrastructure development in Indonesia is not evenly distributed, it is most likely that the location of Indonesian firms also has an influence on their export behaviour.

In the context of Indonesia, significant geographic variations and wide discrepancies in infrastructure and economic development have led to a stark contrast between urban and rural areas. Firms in the urban areas, are presumed to benefit more from the advantage of economical transportation and large pools of skilled labour that contribute to high product quality as compared to those firms located in rural areas. Therefore, manufacturing SMEs in the urban areas should be able to sell their products more easily to foreign markets than firms located in rural areas. Apart from the above advantages, firms in urban areas gain the benefit of close proximity to centres of information and various export stimuli (Dicken and Lloyd, 1990; Knight and Gappert, 1989, Wiedersheim-Paul et al. 1978; Zhao and Zou, 2002), including export promotion programs. These in turn, develop a "positive feedback" (Arthur, 1990) and affect their perceived export benefits and export barriers. Further, cities offer a wider range of business services (accounting, legal, consulting, etc.) than those found in rural areas, which can then improve the chances that businesses will survive and succeed (Mittelstaedt et al. 2006). Based on the above discussion, it can be hypothesized that:

H8: Firm's location has a negative effect on the level of export development, thus having a negative effect on export propensity and intensity.

Following Mittelstaedt et al. (2006), district (a *kabupaten* in Indonesian) populations will be used as the indicator of urbanisation. District populations will be drawn from Indonesian Statistics' estimates. The effect of firm location will be measured based on the industry and trade services data of the existing industrial clusters and/or industrial estate locations in each province.

3.3.3 Dependent Variables

3.3.3.1 SMEs Export Development

This study defines exporting as the transfer of goods across national boundaries using direct and indirect methods (Leonidou and Katsikeas, 1996). The definition includes 'indirect method' because, as highlighted by other studies (see for example Hassler, 2003; Berry et al. 2002; Sjoholm, 2003; Lecraw, 1993), most Indonesian manufacturing SMEs tend to rely on distribution channels or foreign networks in initiating export operations. Therefore, firms engaged both in direct exporting by using their own export departments or divisions, and indirect exporting by relying on distribution channels are considered as exporters in this study.

As supported in the literature, the most effective and viable approach in studying the export behaviour of firms is to classify them by their stage of export development (Bilkey and Tesar, 1977; Czinkota and Johnston, 1981; Reid, 1981). A review of literature on the export development process shows that a wide range of studies has examined the differences between firms based on different stages of export development. However, it also reveals wide inconsistencies in terms of the number of stages of export development proposed by researchers. The number of stages varies from as low as two to as many as six. At the broadest level firms are divided into two main categories, namely non-exporter and exporter (see for example: Westhead, 1995; Keng and Jiuan, 1989; Yaprak, 1985; Kedia and

Chhokar, 1985; Malekzadeh and Nahavandi, 1985). In a cross-sectional study, this division does not discriminate effectively between firms at different stages of the process. Leonidou and Katsikeas (1996), however, take the middle stream by concluding that the export development process can be broadly classified into three major phases. The first phase is the pre-engagement phase, where firms are not exporting. The second phase is the initial phase, where firms are exporting on a marginal basis. The third phase is the advanced phase which includes firms that export on a regular basis and are considering more committed forms of international involvement.

Drawing on the Leonidou and Katsikeas (1996) and Suarez-Ortega (2003) research, this study divides firms into four levels of export development: two levels of non-exporting firms (according to their intention to engage in export activity) and two of exporting firms (according to their levels of export intensity). This segmentation encompasses the following types of firms:

1) The uninterested non-exporters
2) The interested non-exporters
3) The initial exporters
4) The experienced exporters.

The above segmentation scheme supports the generally accepted proposition that exporting is a gradual sequential process with discernible differences between firms at different stages of export development and this process has been shown to be empirically valid across a wide range of studies and within the context of selected firm and managerial characteristics (Yaprak, 1985; Sharkey et al. 1989; Leonidou et al, 1998). Thus, because there is a sufficient number of small and medium sized enterprises involved in exporting in Indonesia, by grouping them into more specific segments, important information or attributes such as intention to initiate or expand export operations (see for example: Gipsrud, 1990; Reid,

1983; Yang et al. 1992) and their propensity to become exporters can be incorporated (Suarez-Ortega and Alamo-Vera, 2005).

In order to categorise firms into the above groups, firstly, the respondents will be asked to choose among five possible states (Leonidou and Katsikeas, 1996; Suarez-Ortega, 2003) that best described their company with respect to export activity, following a self-clustering process (see Table 3.2). Suarez-Ortega argued that this first question is useful in separating the firms based on their self-assessment and it is useful to cross-check the response reliability of any dependent variables used. Secondly, firms have to indicate their export intensity – export sales to total sales ratio- in the last three years. Finally, all firms will be asked whether their company has any intention of initiating or expanding their export operations over the next two years, with 'yes' or 'no' being the two alternative responses. These responses will be dummy coded (1 = if "yes", and 2 = if "no").

Table 3.2 Firms Export Situation

Export situation statements:
1. Your firm has never exported and has no intention to do so in the near future
2. Your firm has never exported but is interested in starting to export
3. Your firm has exported marginally, but the experience has been somewhat disappointing
4. Your firm has had profitable export experiences, but is only taking the first steps towards international markets
5. Your firm is an experienced exporter

Source: Derived from survey data

Note that the specification of export intention in this study follows that of Yang et al. (1992) in using an intention within a two-year period rather than as an immediate course of action. The logical explanation for such classification is that some firms may become involved in exporting fortuitously by responding to unsolicited enquiries from buyers abroad and show no obvious signs of commitment or intention to become an exporter (Suarez-Ortega, 2005). Using this type of classification also accommodates the apparent inconsistency between export attitude and behaviour (Eshghi, 1992).

The responses to the above questions will be used to sort firms into four groups representing four different levels of export commitment. First, exporters are those firms in states 4 and 5, plus firms in state 3 who have nominated an intention to expand export activity in the next two years. The remaining firms are considered non-exporters. Second, among exporters, the study distinguishes between intensive exporters as those firms with an export-to-total sales ratio equal to or greater than 50 per cent, and non-intensive exporters as being the rest (Leonidou, 1998). Finally among non-exporters, the study distinguishes between uninterested and interested non-exporters. Uninterested non-exporters are those firms in state 1 plus firms in state 3 that nominate no intention to engage in exporting in the next two years. Interested non-exporters are those firms in state 2 that nominate an intention to engage in exporting in the next two years.

3.3.3.2 SMEs' Export Intensity

Export intensity is a measure used to quantify the contribution made to a firm's total business by exports (Kirpalani and Balcome, 1987). This ratio is repeatedly used in the export literature as an indicator of a firm's export performance or success (Aaby and Slater, 1989; Leonidou, 1998). It is concluded that the higher the export intensity, the greater the degree of internationalisation. For this study's purpose, and drawing on Leonidou's work (1998), firms with an export-to-total sales ratio equal or greater than 50 per cent will be designated as intensive exporters, and the remaining as non-intensive exporters.

Export intensity will be measured by two items: 1) the percentage of annual sales derived from exports in the most recent financial year; and 2) the percentage of annual sales derived from exports over the last three financial years. According to Anderson (1993), the increase in sales is an indicator of an increased commitment to export markets (Anderson, 1993).

3.3.3.3 SMEs' Export propensity

Many studies have attempted to explain why some firms do not export while others are engaged in exporting by finding a number of differences between exporters and non exporters. Similarly the present study will analyse the propensity for non-exporter SMEs to become exporters by comparing mean values differences of interested non-exporters and initial exporters.

Built on Patterson et al.'s (1999) and Lages and Montgomery's (2004) approaches, export propensity in this study is measured by means of three items focusing on:

1) The likelihood that the company will be exporting its product(s) in the next two years.
2) The desire for the company to export its product(s) in the next two years.

The variable of export propensity will be measured by evaluating the likelihood of a firm to export its product within the next two years. A five-points Likert scale from "Very unlikely" (1), "Unlikely" (2), "Moderate chance" (3), "Likely" (4), to "Very likely" (5) will be used to analyse the variable.

3.4 Data Sources and Description

The secondary data used in the analysis was obtained mainly from Industry and Trade Services in the provinces of Jakarta, West Java, Central Java, and D.I. Yogyakarta; Indonesian Ministry of Cooperative, Small and Medium Enterprises (MOCSME); and the Directorate General for National Export Development (DGNED). Other sources of secondary data were from Indonesian Board of Statistics (*Badan Pusat Statistik* in Indonesian), the business directory of the Indonesian Coordination Board of Investment (*Badan Koordinasi Penanaman Modal* in Indonesia) and the Indonesian yellow pages.

3.4.1 Survey Area

The study focused on four areas of Java Island being: the capital of DKI Jakarta province; West Java province, with the capital of Bandung situated very close to the Indonesian capital, Jakarta; Central Java, with the capital of Semarang; and East Java with the capital of Surabaya. These areas were chosen based on the consideration that they represented some of most densely concentrated areas of SMEs in Indonesia. Of firms with legal entities and registered with Industry and Trade Services through license or permit to establish a firm and business tax file number, the four chosen provinces represent 70.8 per cent of all firms:

The selected four provinces of Central Java, D.K.I Jakarta, East Java, and West Java are considered to be representative due to their higher number of exporting firms than other provinces in Indonesia. This was confirmed through the number of export licenses or export permits obtained from the Directorate General for National for Export Development (abbreviated herein, henceforth DGNED) database.

Table 3.3: Number of Firms Registered with Industry and Trade Services, 2017

	PROVINCE	NUMBER OF FIRMS
1	BALI	605
2	BANTEN	1893
3	BENGKULU	20
4	CENTRAL JAVA	3771
5	CENTRAL KALIMANTAN	80
6	CENTRAL SULAWESI	53
7	D. I. YOGYAKARTA	404
8	D. K. I. JAKARTA	2172
9	EAST JAVA	4941
10	EAST KALIMANTAN	133
11	JAMBI	129
12	LAMPUNG	250
13	MALUKU AND PAPUA	88
14	NORTH SULAWESI	82
15	NORTH SUMATRA	993
16	RIAU AND KEPULAUAN RIAU	371
17	SOUTH EAST SULAWESI	99
18	SOUTH KALIMANTAN	137
19	SOUTH SULAWESI	287
20	SOUTH SUMATRA	282
21	WEST JAVA	4911
22	WEST KALIMANTAN	161
23	WEST NUSA TENGGARA	155
24	WEST SUMATRA	282

Source : DGNED's website, 2017.

Table 3.4: Number of Exporters in All Provinces, 2017

	PROVINCE	NUMBER OF FIRMS
1	BALI	61
2	BANTEN	28
3	BENGKULU	5
4	CENTRAL JAVA	136
5	CENTRAL KALIMANTAN	1
6	CENTRAL SULAWESI	1
7	D. I. YOGYAKARTA	54
8	D. K. I. JAKARTA	234
9	EAST JAVA	70
10	EAST KALIMANTAN	19
11	JAMBI	4
12	LAMPUNG	20
13	MALUKU	8
14	NORTH SULAWESI	5
15	NORTH SUMATRA	39
16	PAPUA	12
17	RIAU	10
18	RIAU ISLAND	11
19	SOUTH EAST SULAWESI	14
20	SOUTH KALIMANTAN	7
21	SOUTH SULAWESI	16
22	SOUTH SUMATRA	12
23	WEST JAVA	139
24	WEST KALIMANTAN	4
25	WEST NUSA TENGGARA	4
26	WEST SUMATRA	16

Source : DGNED's website, 2017.

3.4.2 Population and Sampling Frame

The sample population in this study is small and medium sized firms dealing in exportable manufactured products. The types of industries included are food and beverages, garments and footwear, furniture and wood products. The main reason for targeting these industries is because most of the small and medium sized firms involved in exporting in Indonesia fall under these three industries (Berry et al. 2001). These industries can also be generalized as light industries or consumer goods industries which can offer a better platform for export initiation, particularly in the context of developing countries (Ibeh and Young, 2001; and Tybout, 2000; Wade, 2003).

The sampling frame is developed based on the multiplicity of sources, mentioned in Section 3.4 introduction and 3.4.1, in order to achieve the most comprehensive list possible. Any duplication in the listings was noted and deleted in order to come up with a complete list of SMEs from the three industries and to avoid double counting. However, due to inconsistency in definitions between the Indonesian public agencies and this study, the total number of SMEs has not been categorically identified. The number of firms of all sizes currently registered in the four provinces chosen was 11,258 units (2,172 firms in DKI Jakarta; 4,911 firms in West Java; 3,771 firms in Central Java; and 4941 firms in East Java). The following criteria are used to select firms into the final sampling frames:

1. Firms must meet the criteria of Indonesian SMEs. All other sizes beyond this criteria will be excluded from the analysis.
2. Firms must be producing and/or trading in an exportable product and come from the garments or footwear or wood products sub-sectors. All firms engaged in sub-sectors other than the abovementioned three, as well as firms in the service sector, are excluded.
3. Firms must be privately owned and the owners must be actively involved in the running of the business. Government owned enterprises are not included in the sample.
4. Firms must have been in operation for at least three years.

3.4.3 Sampling Method and Sample Size

Stratified random sampling was used to come up with the final sample population. Malhotra et al. (2002) defined stratified sampling as a two-step process in which the population is partitioned into sub-populations or strata. The strata should be mutually exclusive and collectively exhaustive in that every population element should be assigned to one and only one stratum and no population elements should be omitted. In this study, firms of all sizes currently registered in the four provinces and three industries selected will be firstly stratified along a small, medium, and large sizes stratum, and then through an exporter and non-exporter stratum, and then finally, a simple random sample was taken from each stratum. The two main reasons for using this mixed method are: a) to make the sample more representative and hence improve the precision of the results; b) to achieve greater statistical significance in a smaller sample and reduce the standard error (Malhotra et al., 2002). The same sampling fraction or proportional allocation was taken from each stratum (Cavana et al. 2001). The total number of exporters registered by DGNED is 930 with 408 inclusive of the four provinces and three industries chosen.

The decision on the final size of independent observations (N) required to obtain a sample pattern that is stable and approximates the population involves several issues of consideration. Some researchers typically recommend that the necessary sample size is determined by a set of observed variables (p) involved in the research problem (See for example: Baggaley, 1982; Brislin et al. 1974; Cattell, 1978; Gorsuch, 1983; Hair et al. 1998; Kunce et al. 1975; Lindeman et al. 1980; Marascuilo and Levin; Nunally, 1978). These sources suggest N-to-p ratios which vary from 2:1 to 20:1. A minimum N of 100 to 200 observations is also frequently suggested (Comrey, 1978; Gorsuch, 1983; Guilford, 1954; Hair et al. 1998; Lindeman et al. 1980; Loo, 1983). Velicer et al. (1982), in a simulation study, compared the solutions obtained from three types of factor analysis procedures (principal-components analysis, image-component analysis, and maximum likelihood factor analysis) to determine under what conditions the methods produce different patterns. A comparison of sample factor and component patterns suggested that "with only moderate sample sizes (N = 144), the fit of the pattern to the population target was quite good" (Velicer et al. 1982, p. 386).

In addition to the number of observed variables and the proposed data analysis, Miaoulis and Michener (1976) point out the importance of the level of precision, the level of confidence or risk, and the degree of variability in the attributes being measured. The level of precision or sampling error is defined as the range in which the true value of the population is estimated to be. This range is often expressed in percentage points (for example, ±5 per cent). The confidence level or risk level is based on the key concept encompassed in the Central Limit Theorem. According to this theorem, when a population is repeatedly sampled, the average value of the attribute obtained by those samples is equal to the true population value. The values obtained by these samples are distributed normally about the true value, with some samples obtaining a higher value and some gaining a lower score than the true population value. In a normal distribution, approximately 95% of the sample values are within two standard deviations of the true population value. The degree of variability refers to the distribution of attributes in the population. The more heterogeneous a population, the larger the sample size required to obtain a given level of precision. The more homogeneous a population, the smaller will be the requisite sample size. The degree of variability of 50%, however, suggests a greater level of variability than either 20% or 80%, because 20% or 80% indicate that a large majority do not or do, respectively, have the attribute of interest. The maximum variability of 0.5, therefore, is often used to determine a more conservative sample size which requires a larger sample in order to fit the true variability of the population.

The above criteria are used by various studies developed to estimate sample size. Cochran (1963:75), for example, developed an equation [3] to obtain a representative sample for proportions from a population that is large,

$$n_0 = \frac{Z^2 pq}{e^2} \qquad [3]$$

where n_0 is the sample size, Z^2 is the abscissa of the normal curve that cuts off an area at the tails (the desired confidence level, for example, 95%), e is the desired level of precision, p is the estimated proportion of an attribute that is present in the population, and q is 1-p. Thus, suppose this study intends to estimate the sample from a large population of which variability is unknown, therefore, it is assumed that p=0.5 (maximum variability), and if the study desires a 95% confidence level and ±5% precision, then the sample size will be:

$$n_0 = \frac{Z^2 pq}{e^2} = \frac{(1.96)^2(0.5)(0.5)}{(0.05)^2} = 385$$

If the population is small then the sample size can be reduced slightly. The reduction is carried out when the sample size provides proportionately more information for a small population than a large population, as in the case of an homogeneous population. The sample size (n_0) can be modified using:

$$n = \frac{n_0}{1 + \left(\frac{n_0 - 1}{N}\right)} \qquad [4]$$

Given that the evaluation of this study will only affect 816 exporters and non-exporters, then the sample size would be:

$$n = \frac{n_0}{1 + \left(\frac{n_0 - 1}{N}\right)} = \frac{385}{1 + \left(\frac{385 - 1}{816}\right)} = 261$$

Based on the above result, this study aims to interview 262 exporting and non-exporting firms. However, due to the possibility of a non-response rate which is typically between 60 and 50 per cent for personally administered questionnaires (Groves, 1989; Ornstein, 1998; Massey et al. 1997), then 435 identified exporters and non-exporters in the three industries in the four selected provinces will be targeted for final data collection. This is obtained from the following equation:

$$n^a = \frac{n \times 100}{re\%} = \frac{261 \times 100}{60} = 435$$

Where n^a is the actual sample size required, n is the minimum sample size and re% is the estimated response rate expressed as a percentage (Saunder et al. 2003).

3.4.4 Data Collection Methods

3.4.4.1 Personally Administered Questionnaire Approach

For primary data, a personally administered questionnaire was employed to achieve higher respondent participation and better quality data. During the process of data collection, it is important to select the most appropriate individual in each participant firm to provide the information needed. Most knowledgeable individuals or key informants will be either the export manager (especially in larger firms) or the owner/director (mainly in smaller firms) in order that they have access to the information required by the study. The questionnaire administration was conducted by the author, and emphasis was given to minimising the chance of interviewer bias by designing and implementing a structured questionnaire which was based mainly on a scale format for participant responses.

3.4.4.2 Data Collection Procedure

The data was collected using a personally-administered questionnaire. The questionnaire was designed based on the information needed to test the hypothesis put forward in this study, as well as other issues closely related to exporting. A single questionnaire was designed for both exporters and non-exporters. Most of the questions in the questionnaire make use of five-point Likert and itemised scales, where respondents were asked to tick their responses on clearly outlined alternatives. Such questions make it easier for respondents to fill in the questionnaire, and are also faster than other methods of data collection. The questionnaire also facilitated analysis of data regarding respondent attitudes and opinions using statistical tools such as Statistical Package for Social Science (SPSS) or Analysis of Moment Structure (AMOS).

An information letter was sent before the researcher's visit and administration of the questionnaire. This provided information to the potential respondents regarding the general purpose of the research, as well as inviting their participation and cooperation in the data collection process. It assured them that they would remain anonymous as personal and business identification details were not required. They were informed that, as a requirement of the University of Newcastle Research Ethics Clearance, they could withdraw from the research project at any stage without penalty or register any complaint via the contact details provided in the covering letter.

During the pilot study, the questionnaire was given to officials from DGNED in order to solicit their comments and observations on the questionnaire in general and the issues covered. The aim was to ensure the directorate general was apprised of those issues and considered them to be of real concern and worthy of addressing in the development and promotion of export in small and medium sized firms. The questionnaire was pre-tested on a small sample of 24 firms (12 exporters and 12 non-exporters). The pre-testing aimed to determine if the questionnaire was easily understood by the respondents and to determine the average length of time taken to complete a questionnaire. Personally-administered questionnaire interviews were used to perform the pre-testing and the actual administration of the questionnaire. This not only helped in reducing misunderstood questions and inappropriate or incomplete responses, but also in gaining greater control over the environment in which the survey was administered. In order to help improve the face and content validity of the measures and the study as a whole, respondents in the pre-testing stage were asked to provide comments on the questions. All the observations obtained during the pre-testing stage were taken into account when developing the final questionnaire, which was used in this study.

In administering the final questionnaire, each of the potential respondents was contacted and personally interviewed based on the structured questions in the questionnaire. Personal physical presence was considered important because it was strongly believed that most of the respondents would not be keen to fill out the questionnaire without help and guidance from the interviewer. Physical presence therefore, was expected to improve the response rate. The over-reliance on mail out surveys by most of the previous studies (Bell and Young, 1998), which achieved low response rates, also justifies the use of a mixed methods approach.

3.5 Statistical Techniques for Data Analysis

All the data collected in this study was subject to statistical analysis using Statistical Package for Social Science (SPSS) and Analysis of Moment Structure (AMOS). The five-point Likert and itemised scales were treated as interval scales. Diamantopoulos and Schlegelmilch (1997) pointed out that Likert scales, semantic differential scales, itemised rating scales, as well as Stapel scales, can be considered interval scales, especially in social research. Cavana et al. (2001) noted that, in some cases, numbers can be assigned to the different categories in a categorical scale and as long as the intervals between each category are equal, then the scales can be treated as interval. The scales were tested for their reliability and validity before using them in the analysis.

3.5.1 Univariate and Multivariate Data Processing and Analysis

Data processing and analysis techniques will include:

1) Descriptive Statistics – Descriptive statistics are used to describe the sample of concern. They are used to identify patterns and general trends in a data set. Together with simple graphics analysis, they form the basis of every quantitative analysis of data. Descriptive statistics are typically distinguished from inferential statistics. Descriptive statistics simply describe what the data shows, while inferential statistics are designed to reach conclusions that extend beyond the immediate data alone (Berenson and Levine, 1983).

   One such descriptive technique is univariate analysis, which examines one variable at a time. There are three major characteristics of a single variable that are frequently analysed: a) the distribution (variable frequency counts, percentages, cumulative percentages); b) the central tendency (mean, median, mode); and c) the dispersion (standard deviation). All of these characteristics for each of the internal and external determinants of export development will be described in the analysis and presentation of findings.

2) Chi-square Test – The Chi-square test will be used as a substitute t-test in cases where testing for differences involves variables that are purely categorical. There are a number of predictor variables that are characterized as categorical variables, for example: gender, intention to export. To examine hypothesis using such variables, the chi-square test will be used.

   The chi-square test is used in two similar but distinct circumstances:

a) For estimating how closely an observed distribution matches an expected distribution – this is usually referred to as the goodness-of-fit-test;

b) For estimating whether two random variables are independent.

In addition to the chi-square test, a number of other model fit indices will be used to determine whether the observed data supports the hypothesized model in this factor analysis. An assessment of model fit determines the degree to which parameter estimates of the proposed model are able to reproduce the sample data variance and covariance. Usually, model evaluation is assessed by the chi-square test and its accompanying significance test. If the associated *p* value *is not significant*, one can conclude that there is no significant difference between the sample variance/covariance matrix and the model-implied variance/covariance matrix and hence the data fits the model well.

The most common indices found in the literature are CMIN/DF, the Standardized Root-Mean-Square Residual (SRMR), the Root Mean Square Error of Approximation (RMSEA), the Goodness-of-fit Index (GFI), the Adjusted Goodness-of-fit Index (AGFI), the Normed Fit Index (NFI), the Tucker-Lewis index (TLI), and the Comparative Fit Index (CFI). The properties of these fit indices will be briefly discussed in the following sub-sections.

a) CMIN/DF is the minimum discrepancy divided by its degrees of freedom. Several writers (see for example Wheaton et al., 1977; Carmines and McIver, 1981; Marsh and Hocevar, 1985) suggested ratios in the range of 2 to 1 or 3 to 1 as indications of an acceptable fit between the hypothetical model and the sample data.

b) The Standardized Root-Mean-Square Residual (RMR) measures the average difference between corresponding elements of the sample and model-implied correlation matrices. Because the units of measurement are in standardized form, a model may be considered to fit the data well when this average value is less than 0.05 (Hu and Bentler, 1999). Large values of the SRMR may indicate outliers in the data.

c) The Root-Mean-Square Error of Approximation (RMSEA) – The logic underlying RMSEA is that no model will ever fit exactly in the population and one can only rely on a close approximation to reality (Browne and Cudeck in Bollen and Long, 1993). The RMSEA computation requires the chi-square statistic, degrees of freedom, and sample size for the target model (Rigdon, 1996). The RMSEA has a lower bound of zero which indicates a perfect fit with values increasing as model fit deteriorates. Browne and Cudeck in Bollen and Long (1993) suggested that a RMSEA value of about 0.05 or less indicates a model of close fit, while values between 0.05 and 0.08 indicate reasonable fit.

d) The Goodness-of-fit index (GFI) and the Adjusted Goodness-of-fit index (AGFI) provide an indication of the relative amounts of the covariance among the latent variables that are accounted for by the model (Mathieu et al., 1992). The GFI is based on a ratio of the sum of the squared differences between the observed and reproduced matrices to the observed variances. The AGFI is the GFI adjusted for the degrees of freedom of the model relative to the number of variables. Both the GFI and AGFI should be between 0 and 1 with values exceeding 0.95 considered to be an indication that the data fits a model well.

e) NFI or normed fit index incorporates the minimum discrepancy of the model being evaluated and the minimum discrepancy of the baseline model (Bentler and Bonett, 1980). Models with overall fit indices of less than 0.90 can usually be improved substantially.

f) TLI or Tucker-Lewis index estimates the relative improvement per degree of freedom of the target model over an independence model (Hu and

Bentler, 1998). For a good fitting model, values exceeding 0.95 are preferred.

g) CFI or comparative fit index measures the improvement in going from a target model to an independence model. The CFI has a range of 0-1 and values greater than 0.95 are generally considered satisfactory fit of the model to the data (Hu and Bentler, 1999).

3) Correlation Analysis – Using correlation coefficients, correlation analysis will be used to test for statistical association of variables. It allows for measurement of a linear association between two variables. Values of the correlation coefficient are always between -1 and +1. A correlation coefficient of +1 indicates that the two variables are perfectly related in a positive linear sense; a correlation coefficient of -1 indicates that the two variables are perfectly related in a negative linear sense; and a correlation coefficient of 0 indicates that there is no linear relationship between the two variables.

For simple linear regression, the sample correlation coefficient is the square root of the coefficient of determination. Correlation analysis will be extensively used in testing the correlation between each independent variable and dependent variable in the proposed model. The firm size variable, for instance, will be tested to investigate whether it has a positive or negative correlation with the level of export development.

4) Path Analysis – Path analysis will be used to examine multiple relationships in a single model. Path analysis will be used as an alternative to multiple regressions which can estimate a single relationship. However, path analysis in AMOS can estimate many equations at once (Hair et al. 1998).

Other advantages of path analysis compared to multiple regression include more flexible assumptions (particularly allowing interpretation even in the face of multicollinearity), use of confirmatory factor analysis to reduce measurement error by having multiple indicators per latent variable (Loehlin, 1992), the support of path analysis' graphical modelling interface, the desirability of testing models overall rather than coefficients individually (Madigan and Raftery, 1994), the ability to test models with multiple dependents, the ability to model mediating variables, the ability to model error terms (Kline, 1998), the ability to test coefficients across multiple between-subjects groups, and the ability to handle difficult data (time series with autocorrelated error, non-normal data, incomplete data) (Olsson et al. 2000).

Nevertheless path analysis, using AMOS software, remains limited to continuous dependent variables. The non-metric character of a dichotomous dependent variable is accommodated by making predictions of group membership based on Z scores. AMOS approaches this task in a manner similar to that found in logistic regression and multiple regression analysis. Structural equation modelling also cannot itself draw causal arrows in models or resolve causal ambiguities. Theoretical insight and judgment by the researcher, therefore, are still of utmost importance (Hair et al. 1998).

3.6 Chapter Summary

In this chapter, the research design and methodology of the study have been discussed and the focus has been on making operational the independent and dependent variables as well as constructing the hypotheses that will be tested by the study. The chapter also outlines the sampling plan, data collection methods, and statistical techniques used for analysing the data.

The export development construct is presented as a categorical variable consisting of four categories; the uninterested non-exporters, the interested non-exporters, the initial exporters, and the experienced exporters. To validate this segmentation approach, other dependent variables of export intention, export propensity, and export intensity are also utilised. In terms of factors that determine the export development of a firm, a number of internal determinants and one external determinant have been included in the analysis. These factors are firm specific resources and capabilities, management background characteristics, and export promotion programs. The proposed export development model and its mathematical equation form are aimed at understanding the relationships of numerous factors associated with the export development process of a firm.

Due to a lack of a readily available sampling frame in the chosen industries, a sampling frame is developed with the help of lists from Industry and Trade Services in the provinces of West Java, Central Java, and Special Province of Yogyakarta; plus the Ministry of Cooperative, and Small and Medium Enterprises; Directorate General of National Export Development; and the Central Board of Statistics.

A personally administered questionnaire was the instrument used to collect data. The questionnaire was initially pre-tested on a group of 12 exporting firms and 12 non-exporting firms. In addition, in-depth interviews with the respondents were held at the same time in order to collect more information on issues covered in the questionnaire. Only the owner/part owner managers of the firms were allowed to fill in the questionnaire.

In the following chapters the analysis of the data will be reported. This analysis uses Statistical Package for Social Science (SPSS) and Analysis of Moment Structure (AMOS). A number of statistical techniques are employed including crosstab analysis, chi-square test, standard t-test, correlation, factor analysis and path analysis.

****

CHAPTER FOUR

EMPIRICAL ANALYSIS OF ORGANISATIONAL AND MANAGERIAL CHARACTERISTICS OF MANUFACTURING SMES IN INDONESIA

4.1 Introduction

This chapter reports and discusses the analysis of organisational and managerial characteristics of manufacturing firms in Indonesia. In the recent changing global environment competing firms need to understand the factors that influence their competitive behaviour. This chapter investigates the differences and similarities that exist in organisational, managerial, and export development characteristics between exporting and non-exporting SMEs manufacturing in Indonesia.

The rest of this chapter is organized as follows: Section 4.2 discusses the organisational characteristics of the responding firms. Section .3 examines the managerial characteristics of the responding firms. Section 4.4 explores the distribution of exporting and non-exporting firms by specifying their export development, export propensity, and export intensity variables. Section 4.5 summarizes the findings in the chapter.

4.2 Organisational Characteristics of Manufacturing SMEs in Indonesia

4.2.1 Sub-sector Characteristics of Manufacturing SMEs

Figure 4.1 depicts the sub-sector shares of surveyed manufacturing SMEs in Indonesia in 2008. Of the 197 firms surveyed, 80 firms or 41 per cent are from furniture and wood products, 60 firms or 30 per cent are from garments, and 57 firms or 29 per cent belong to the footwear sub-sector.

Figure 4.1 Sub-sector Distribution of Manufacturing SMEs in Indonesia

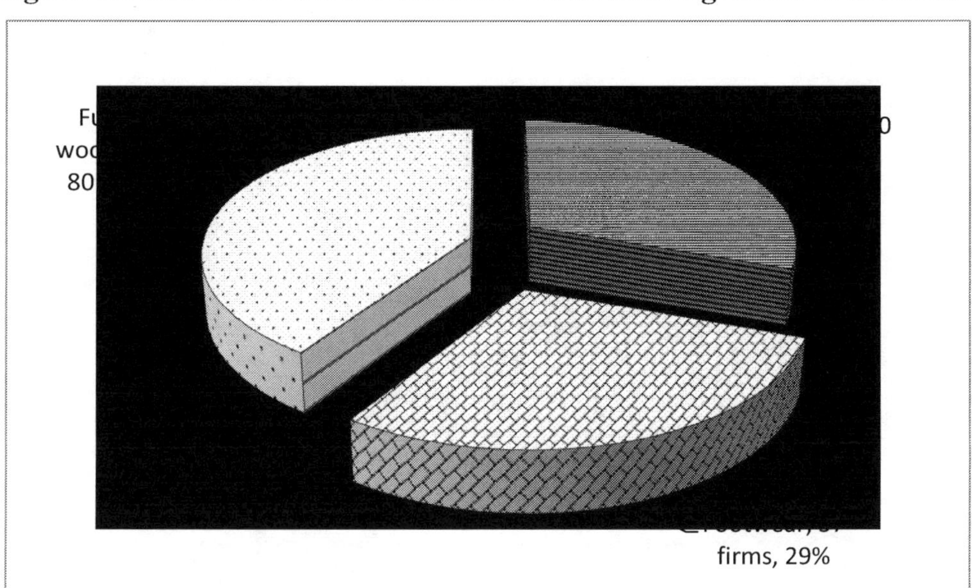

Source: Derived from survey data.

Figure 4.2 depicts the export development within each of the sub-sectors in the manufacturing industry and shows that the majority of exporters are in the furniture and wood products sub-sector. Most of the non-exporters are in the garment and footwear sub-sectors. A possible explanation for this dominance of furniture and wood products in exports is that Indonesian government schemes have aimed at promoting value-added exports of furniture and wood products; consequently, this sub-sector has developed a capability of attracting investment to itself as well as to the relatively unregulated forest sector. This in turn has encouraged the use of non-wood materials and other alternative materials from waste wood or plantation crops (KEMENPERIN, 2017). Therefore, although timber supply from clearing of conversion forests is scheduled to decline, the furniture and wood products sub-sector is able to accommodate to the market conditions by improving quality control and superior design; meeting international environment standards; and enhancing marketing effort in international markets (Aswicahyono & Hill, 2004). Furthermore, despite the fierce competition from countries such as China, Malaysia and Vietnam, Indonesian furniture and wood products are able to maintain their competitive characteristics by producing tropical hard-wood products with unique carving designs (KEMENPERIN, 2017).

Figure 4.2: Manufacturing SMEs by Sub-sector and Share of Export Development (Frequency Distribution)

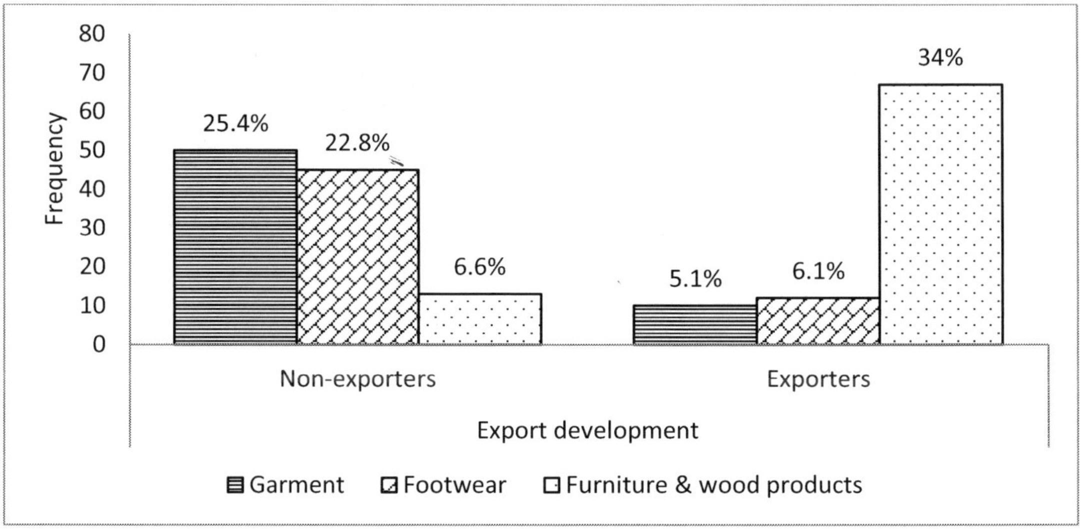

Source: Derived from survey data.

Figure 4.2 puts the garment sub-sector share of exports at 6.1 per cent. A brief overview of recent history offers some context for this weaker performance. Although the garment sub-sector has existed downstream of the textile industry for longer than the wood and furniture sub-sector has existed, it is experiencing declines in exports due to the quota system imposed by the United States to protect Chinese products. Coupled with this, following the Asian financial crisis in 1997, there has been a decline in capital investment in the garment sub-sector, (Akatiga, 2007). Notably, during the period 2000-2005, despite the introduction of the quota system, exports from the garment industry grew steadily in the first half of 2006 by 0.82 percent (Akatiga, 2007).

Again, an historical overview is useful to contextualize the low proportion of footwear exporters. For this sub-sector exports grew in the late 1980s but declined following the financial crisis of 1997, peaking at $US2.2 billion in 1996

(KEMENPERIN, 2017). Following the Asian financial crisis, exports declined dramatically with Indonesia's ranking slipping from 3 to 10, being squeezed by major competitors such as China, India, and Vietnam. Despite this loss in competitiveness, the growth experienced in the global footwear market has meant that there is a potential for Indonesia to regain the competitive edge it achieved prior to the crisis of 1997.

The Pearson Chi-Square (χ^2) test for independence was carried out to find out whether the sub-sector and export development level had a relationship that could be used to explain the distribution above. Prior to performing the test throughout the chapter, the underlying assumptions of the test were investigated. A contingency table generated by SPSS fulfilled the following conditions:

1) Each observation is independent of all the others (that is each subject contributes data to only one cell). Therefore, the sum of all cell frequencies in the table must be the same as the number of subjects in the sample.

2) No more than 20 per cent of the expected counts are less than 5 and all individual expected counts are 1 or greater (Yates, Moore, and McCabe, 1999).

Following the test for independence and given the calculated value of χ^2 (2, N = 197) = 56.40 and a p-value of 0.000 which is less than the critical value of 0.05, the study rejects the null hypotheses and concludes that there is a significant relationship between the sub-sector and the level of export development, at the 5% significance level.

4.2.2 Firm Ownership Structure

Figure 4.3 reveals that out of the 197 respondents, 176 respondents or 89.3 per cent are sole proprietorships. Of the 176 respondents who are sole traders, 32.4 per cent come from garments, 30.7 per cent from footwear, and 36.9 per cent from furniture and wood products. Splitting the sole proprietorships by export development reveals 51.1 per cent are classified as exporters, while 48.9 per cent are non-exporters. Of the garment sub-sector sole proprietorships, 33 per cent are classified exporters while 67 per cent are classified non-exporters. Similarly with the footwear sub-sector, 33 per cent are exporters and 67 per cent are non-exporters. In the furniture and wood products, 87.5 per cent of sole proprietorships are classified exporters and 12.5 per cent are classified non-exporters. Figure 4.3 in addition, shows that there are more exporters (90.5 per cent) than non-exporters (9.5 per cent) in the partnership form of ownership.

Figure 4.3: Manufacturing SMEs by Sub-sector, Ownership and Export Development (Per cent of 197 Firms)

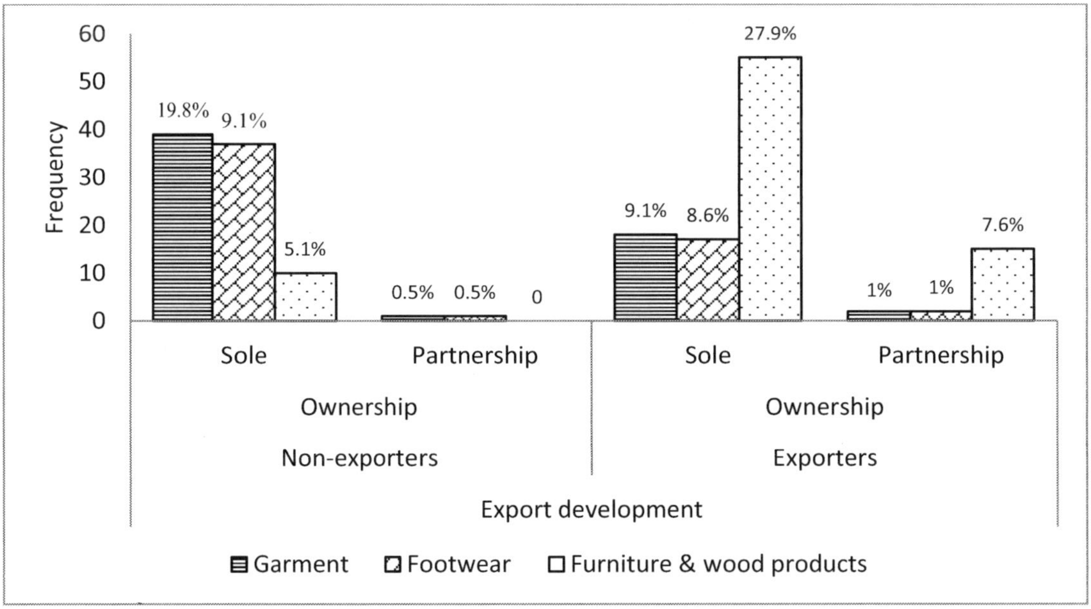

Source: Derived from survey data.

The Chi-Square (χ^2) test for independence was carried out to find out whether firm ownership structure and export development level had a relationship to explain the distribution above. The results from the test for independence showed the calculated value of χ^2 (1, N = 197) = 11.75 and a p-value of 0.001 which is less than the critical value of 0.05. The study therefore rejects the null hypotheses and concludes that there is a significant relationship between firm ownership structure and the level of export development, at the 5% significance level.

The simplicity in establishing and terminating single proprietorships has made this type of legal business structure the most common form of ownership found in Indonesia (Wengel and Rodriguez, 2000; Wibowo, 2007). Opening a sole-proprietor business in Indonesia requires less time and cost associated with registration and licensing than a partnership business (Wengel and Rodriguez, 2000). The difficulty in opening up a partnership business in Indonesia, according to the World Bank (2006), is that it might take 151 days to complete all the paperwork. Thus, it is not surprising that Yudhoyono's administration was committed to cutting down this duration from 150 to 30 days (Presidential Instruction, 2006).

4.2.3 Firm Size Structure

Firm size in this study is measured by the total number of full time employees and the total asset value in Indonesian Rupiah currency. Figure 4.4 depicts the respective frequency distribution of the sample according to the exporter/non-exporter and the sub-sector categories.

Figure 4.4: Manufacturing SMEs by Sub-sector, Export Development and Size of Firm measured in Full Time Employees (Frequency Distribution)

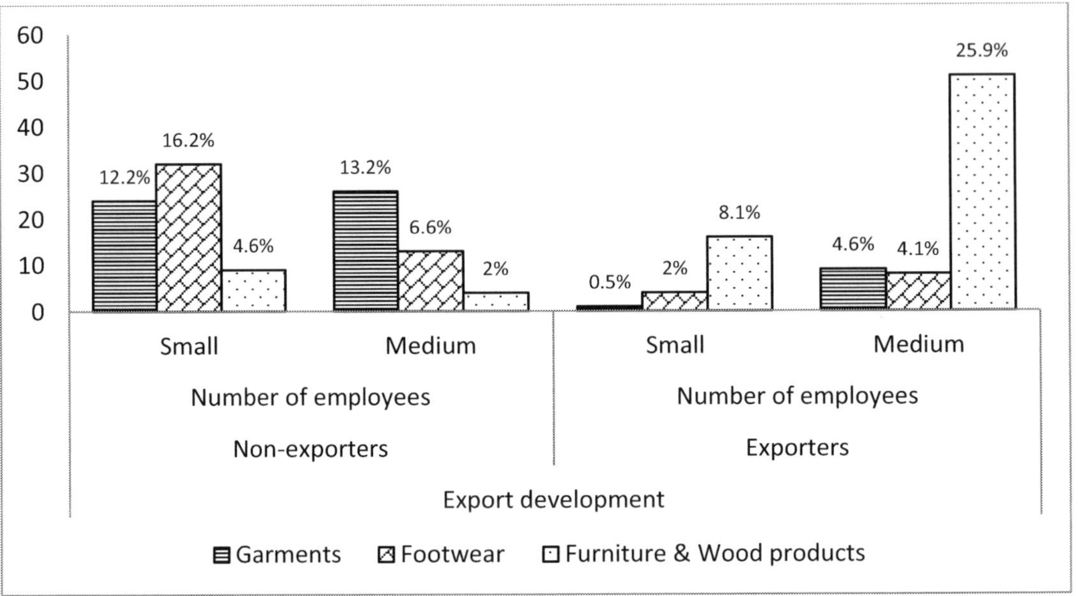

Source: Derived from survey data.

According to Figure 4.4, 86 firms or 44 per cent of the sample are of small size, that is have between 5 and 19 full-time employees, and 111 firms or 56 per cent are of medium size and have between 20 to 300 full time employees. Footwear firms dominate the small sized firms and both garment and footwear firms are predominantly non-exporters. While furniture and wood product firms dominate the medium size category with the majority of firms also exporters.

The Indonesian footwear sub-sector mainly produces labour-intensive and low-skilled products (KEMENPERIN, 2017). Several macro and micro issues such as the emergence of new industry competitors like China, Vietnam, and Thailand; lack of production technology development; and lack of access to financial resources; are maintained to be the main causes that reduce the footwear sub-sector's opportunities to develop into large businesses (KEMENPERIN, 2017).

Within the garment sub-sector, a number of firms have reached an economic scale by combining advanced technology in their machinery with full capacity utilisation of the workforce in their production system (Van Diermen, 1999). Between 1975 and 1991, the garment sub-sector experienced significant structural change, with some firms managing large scale operations employing 1000 workers in their production systems (Australian National University, 1994). However, as noted earlier, the industry has faced problems post the Asian financial crisis of 1997.

The pooled independent sample t-test was carried out to find out whether there was a significant difference between exporters and non-exporters in terms of the average numbers of full-time employees. Prior to performing independent sample t-tests throughout the chapter, the following underlying assumptions of the test were carried out (Coakes et al., 2010):

1) All observations must be independent of each other;
2) The dependent variable must be measured on an interval or ratio scale;
3) The dependent variable must be normally distributed in the population (normality assumption);
4) The distribution of the dependent variable for one of the groups being compared must have the same variance as the distribution for the other group being compared (homogeneity of variance assumption).

The Levene test results from SPSS indicate that the assumption of homogeneity of variance is not supported. Given that an F-value of 36.432 and a p value of 0.000, which is less than the critical value of 0.05, is obtained the Levene's test is significant. When the Levene test is significant, modified procedures that do not assume equality of variance are used (Coakes et al, 2010). Following the t-tests and given the calculated t-value = -5.065 and a p-value of 0.000, which is less than the critical value of 0.05, the study rejects the null hypotheses and concludes that there is significant difference between exporters and non-exporters in the mean of full time employees hired.

The analysis on an individual size, however, shows that significant difference only hold between medium exporting and medium non-exporting firms. The output generated by the SPSS indicates a calculated t-value of -3.323 and a p-value of 0.001, which is less than the critical value of 0.05. The study, then, rejects the null hypotheses and concludes that there is a significant difference between medium-sized exporters and medium-sized non-exporters in the mean of full time employees hired. The difference between small exporting and small non-exporting firms is found to be insignificant at a calculated t-value = -0.322 and a p-value of 0.755, which is more than the critical value of 0.05. The study, therefore, accepts the null hypotheses and concludes that small exporting firms have a relatively similar mean with that of small non-exporting firms in terms of full time employees.

Firm size distribution based on the total asset value (MOCSME' classification) is illustrated in Figure 4.5. One hundred and eleven firms or 56 per cent of all respondents have a total asset value deemed to be medium size and 86 firms or 44 per cent are of small size. As with Figure 4.4, the preponderance of small sized firms in the garment and footwear sub-sectors are non-exporters, while the furniture and wood products sub-sector is biased towards medium sized firms, most of whom are exporters.

Figure 4.5: Manufacturing SMEs by Sub-sector, Export Development and Size of Firm measured in Asset Values (Frequency Distribution)

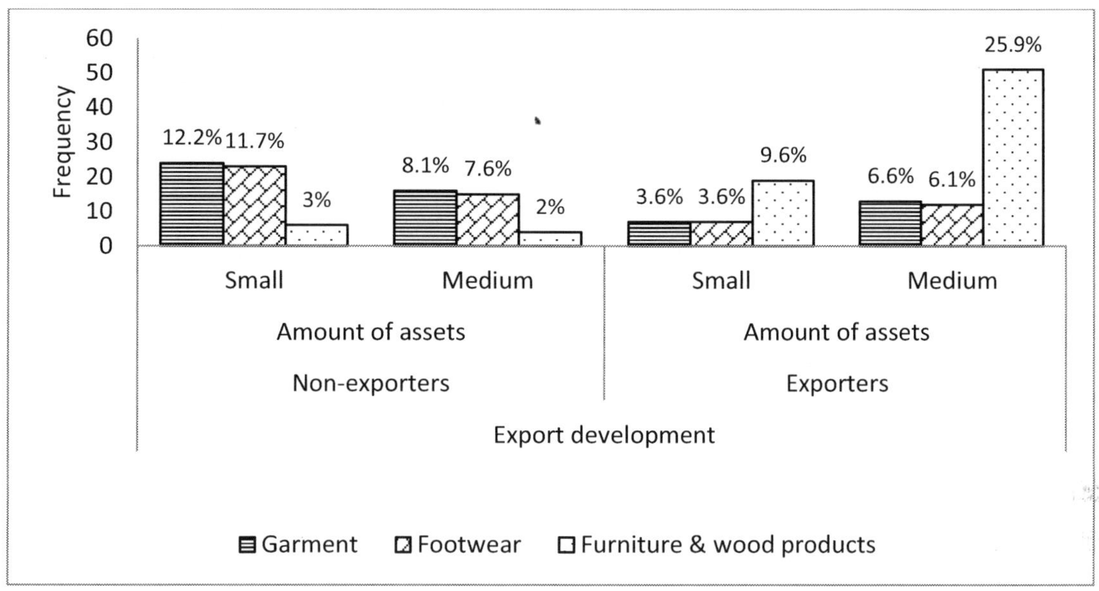

Source: Derived from survey data.

Since the data is on an ordinal scale, the Mann-Whitney U test (Wilcoxon rank sum W test) was used to test the difference between exporters and non-exporters in their mean rank of assets value. Similar to the earlier t-tests, prior to conducting the Mann-Whitney U test throughout the chapter, the following assumptions were examined (Coakes et al., 2010):

1) Random samples from populations
2) Independence within samples and mutual independence between samples
3) Measurement scale is at least ordinal

The results generated by SPSS indicate that the data set has fulfilled all the above assumptions and exporting firms are revealed to have higher mean rank in their assets value (mean rank = 112.7) than that of non-exporting ones (mean rank = 82.1). Thus, given the z-score of -4.316 and the p-value of 0.000, the study rejects the null hypotheses and concludes that there is significant difference between exporter and non-exporter groups in their mean rank of assets owned at 5 percent significance level. The study cannot perform the analysis within each of the individual sizes because the measurement scale for the amount of assets was dummy coded (1= if small-sized firms, and 2 = if medium-sized firms).

The significant difference between exporter and non-exporter groups in the two factor measures above supports the tenet that larger firms do have more flexibility in managerial, financial and production matters that lead them to greater commitments to exporting than smaller firms (Mittelstaedt et al., 2003; Wagner, 2001; Isgut, 2001; Westhead, 1995; Chetty and Hamilton, 1993; Calof, 1993; and Bonaccorsi, 1992). In their study of Indonesian exporting SMEs, Wengel and Rodriguez (2006) found that size does matter in the business of exporting, namely because of the economies of scale in shipping and handling. In order to produce products that meet export standards and designs and to manage the costs associated with international expansion, exporting firms are more likely to seek larger amounts of formal credit and resources than non-exporting firms (Wengel and Rodriguez, 2004; Basri and van der Eng, 2004) and this also explains the significant difference between these two groups in relation to their amount of assets.

4.2.4 Firm Age Structure

Firm age in this study is gauged by length of time a firm had been in operation. Figure 4.6 reveals that 52 per cent of all firms have been in operation for less than 10 years, with 39 per cent being active for 10 to 20 years of operation. Very few firms are aged more that 20 years but of these almost half are garment firms.

Figure 4.6: Manufacturing SMEs by Sub-sector, Export Development and Age of Firm in Years (Frequency Distribution)

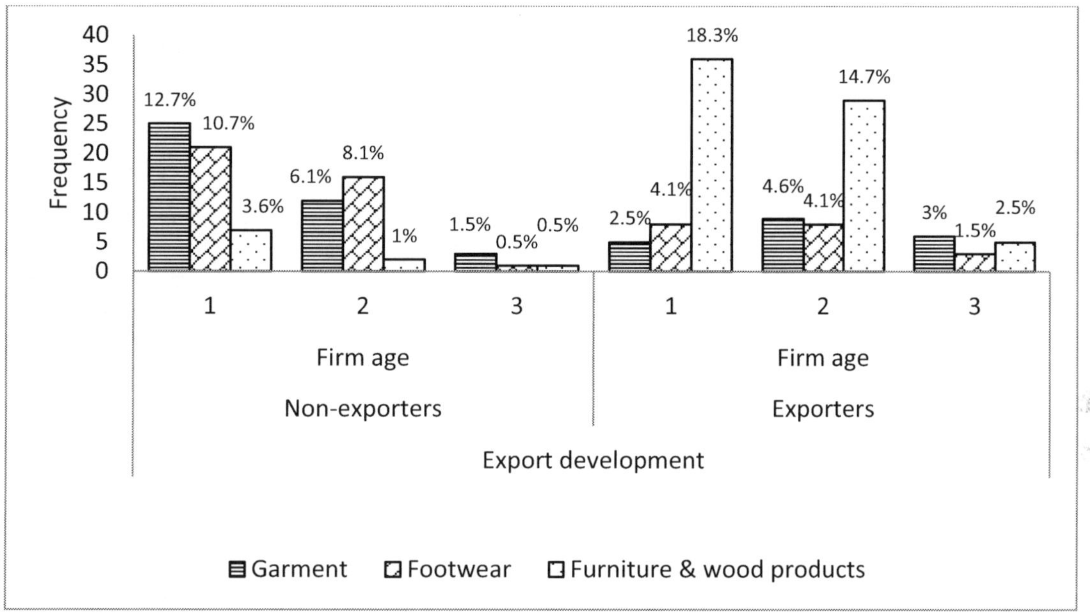

Notes: 1= less than 10 years; 2 = 10 to 20 years; 3 = more than 20 years.
Source: Derived from survey data.

The garment sub-sector is the longest established sub-sectors of the three under consideration. The social science data archives from Australian National University (1994) show that there were 200 garment firms employing an average of 42 workers in 1975. This number continued to increase and reached 1490 firms in 1991 (ANU, 1994). The growth of medium and large sized enterprises, however, slowed down between 1985 and 1988 (Van Diermen, 1990). The fact that the exporting firms are substantially from wood and furniture products and drawn from the younger age groups might also provide evidence of the country's belated export orientation pattern that has only been embraced and supported explicitly by the government since the mid-1980s (Soesastro and Basri, 2005).

The results from the pooled standard t-test indicate that there is a significant difference between exporters and non-exporters in the means of their firm age, at 5 per cent significance level (t-value = -2.288 and p-value = 0.023). A standard t-test shows that the assumptions of homogeneity of variance are supported by Levene's test (F-value = 0.796, p-value = 0.373). The two-tailed significance for firm age indicates that exporting firms have a higher mean in their firm age ($\bar{x}$ = 13.16, s.d.= 7.43) than that of non-exporting firms ($\bar{x}$ = 10.72, s.d.= 7.46). The results are in contrast to Wengel and Rodriguez' study (2006) which found firm's age to be negative and highly significant for small and large enterprises alike. Newly established Indonesian firms in Wengel and Rodriguez' study are found to have greater export orientation than their older counterparts.

4.2.5 Geographic Market Development

Geographic market development in this study indicates area(s) in the domestic market in which a firm is currently marketing its products. Figure 4.7 reveals that very few firms are restricted to local or provincial markets. The greatest concentration of exporting firms (except for the 17 respondents, or 8.6 per cent of firms, who directed their entire output to international markets) operated from one regional area (17.2 per cent of all firms). Non-exporters dominate in the domestic market with 13.1 per cent of all firms compared to exporters with 9.6 per cent.

At the sub-sector level, firms from furniture and wood products are predominantly exporters operating from one or multiple regional markets. Their lower representation in the national market may imply a forsaking of the domestic market in preference for a stronger focus on overseas markets (Johanson and Wiedersheim-Paul, 1975). Firms in the garment and footwear sub-sectors are notably non-exporters. Representation of non-exporting garment firms is greatest in one region markets and the national market; while representation of footwear non-exporters is greatest in multi-regional markets and the national market. The massive contraction of domestic demand and buying power, particularly after the 1997 Asian financial crisis, may have pushed exporters from furniture and wood products to pass on some of the exchange rate depreciation to foreign buyers in order to boost export revenue (Athukorala, 2006).

Figure 4.7: Manufacturing SMEs by Sub-sector, Export Development and Geographic Market Development (Frequency Distribution)

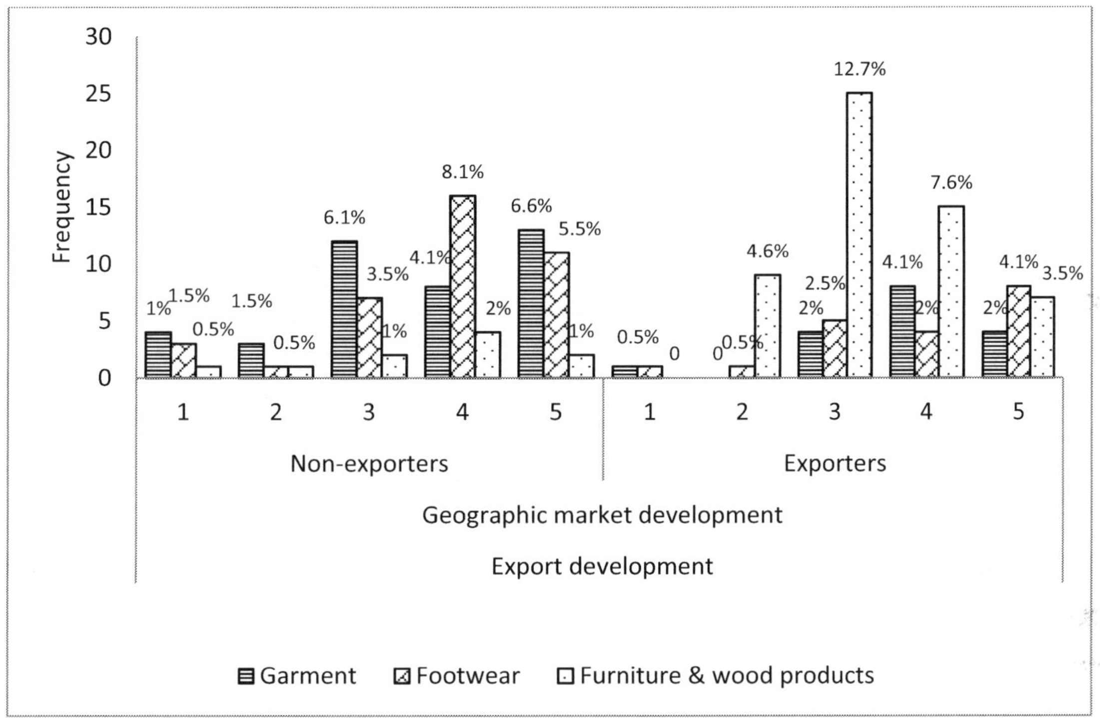

Notes: 1= local market, for example within a district or districts; 2 = provincial market; 3 = regional market, for example western Indonesian region or central Indonesian region; 4 = more than one region market; 5 = nation-wide market.

Source: Derived from survey data.

The Mann-Whitney U test (Wilcoxon rank sum W test) results reveal no significant difference between exporting and non-exporting manufacturers in terms of their geographic market development. Exporting and non-exporting firms were found to have relatively equal mean ranks in their geographic market development (Mean ranks of exporters and non-exporters were 95.22 and 102.06 respectively). The mean difference of geographic market developed by both exporters and non-exporters is found to be insignificant at the 5 per cent significance level as z = -.862 and p = 0.389.

The non-significant results in the above test indicate that geographic market development does not really influence Indonesian SMEs' behaviour in developing their level of export operation. Export intention, defined as the intention of a non-exporter to initiate exporting and the intention of an exporter to expand export operation, is also tested to validate the notion that export initiation is highly associated with growth in the domestic market. The result of the Mann-Whitney U test, however, generates a non-significant mean rank difference between groups with an intention to export (mean rank = 100.41) and groups without an export intention (mean rank = 87.82) at 5 percent significance level as z-score = -1.005 and p-value = 0.315. Hence, prior domestic experience which is said to help firms accumulate knowledge and prepare them to participate in international market opportunities (Suarez-Ortega and Alamo-Vera, 2005; Barkema et al.; 1996; Erramilli, 1991; Cavusgil, 1984; Welch and Wiedersheim-Paul, 1980), may not be an important factor in the Indonesian context as they do not determine a firm's ability to expand to overseas markets.

Although the structures of Indonesian manufacturing industry have changed rapidly toward export orientation, some sub-sectors including the three sub-sectors of the present analysis are still facing a number of export barriers. These are largely reflected in the complex market demands and designs (different markets requirements of quality and design) and other external factors (tariff and non-tariff barriers, free trade area agreements, economic zones) beyond their control. Skills and training of the management and workers, gained in the domestic market, therefore, have not actually endowed them with the capabilities to meet the high quality and design expectations of export markets. The results also raise a question as to the relevance of the training and supports provided by the government, to the needs of SMEs' export development.

4.2.6 Firm Location Distribution

The respondents in the study were asked to indicate the distance of their firms from the nearest first city. The respondents were also requested to specify whether or not their firms were located in an industrial cluster or an industrial estate. Figure 4.8 shows that the majority of the firms (79.7 per cent), irrespective of their level of export development were within 1 to 10 kilometres away from the nearest city centre. A similar pattern occurs at the sub-sector level, with most firms in all sub-sectors located in the vicinity of the city centre. Some firms, mainly from garment and furniture and wood products, located their production facilities further away from the city centre.

A standard t-test shows the assumptions of homogeneity of variance are supported by Levene's test (F-value = 0.141, p-value = 0.708) and the findings show that there is no significant mean difference between exporting firms ($\bar{x}$ = 8.86, s.d.= 9.95) and non-exporting firms ($\bar{x}$ = 8.53, s.d.= 9.18) in terms of their distance from the city centre (t-value = -0.243 and p = 0.808). The validation test, based on the intention to export, shows similar results. The mean of exporters' distance ($\bar{x}$ = 8.78, s.d.= 9.97) was similar to that of non-exporters ($\bar{x}$ = 8.21, s.d.= 5.89) at 5 per cent significance level (t-value = -.258 and p-value = 0.796).

Figure 4.8: Manufacturing SMEs by Sub-sector, Export Development and Proximity to City Centre (Frequency Distribution)

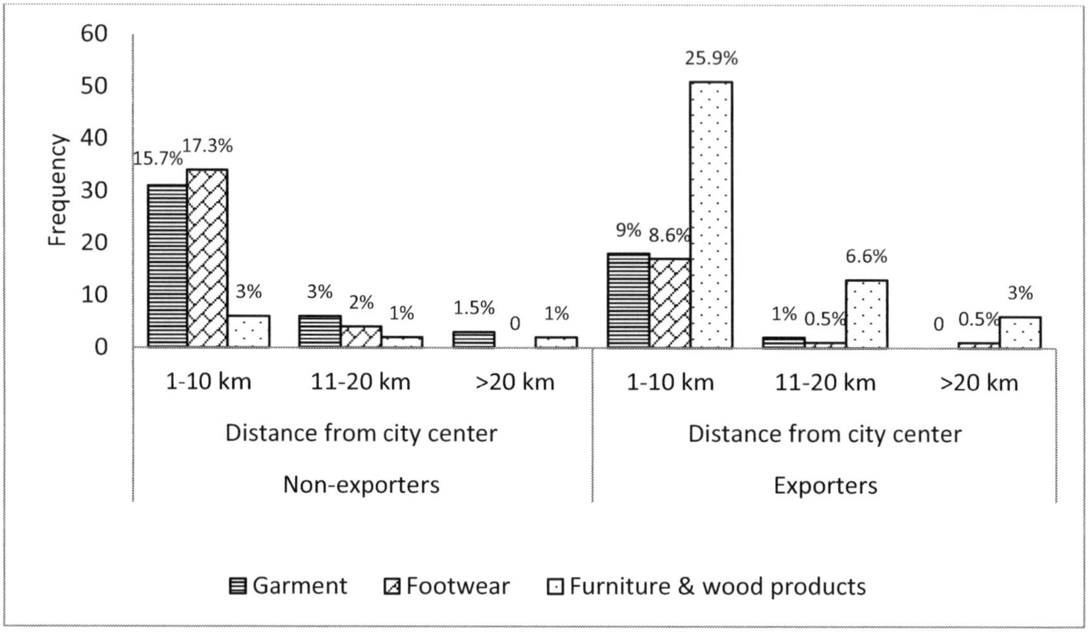

Source: Derived from survey data.

Location measures earlier proved to be insignificant, suggesting that although there are wide discrepancies in infrastructure and economic development between rural and urban areas in Indonesia, they may not be an obstruction to the firm's intention to engage in export operation. Although the role of location in explaining the propensity to export has been extensively discussed by the literature (Mittelstaedt et al., 2006; Zhao and Zou, 2002; Berry et al., 1997; Dicken and Lloyd, 1990; Arthur, 1990), in the light of the above findings, it can be implied that since most firms are located within urban areas, the spiral effects of the localisation economies, such as common service facilities and regional infrastructure, are likely to be shared by both exporting and non-exporting firms. Therefore externalities from both urbanisation and industrial agglomeration may not be considered as important as other externalities that can specifically address and assist individual group's needs based on their level of export development.

These findings, however, are quite the opposite of Tambunan' study (2005) which found clustering or agglomeration approaches an important strategy to develop Indonesian SMEs. From Tambunan's study, industry localisation is important because it assists the government in the provision of support, training, and general facilities.

4.3. Managerial Characteristics of Manufacturing SMEs in Indonesia

4.3.1 Age of the Manager

As described in the methodology chapter, this study assumes demographic or objective managerial characteristics instead of subjective, psychological attributes of management to explain export development of the firm. The management characteristics are: (a) age; (b) level of education; (c) overseas experience; and (d) foreign language proficiency.

As found in Figure 4.9, the majority of managers or owners in both exporting and non-exporting firms are in a relatively mature age group. About 73.6 per cent of respondents are aged 31 to 50 years old. Some 15 per cent of sample firms are managed or owned by people over 50. This pattern holds at the sub-sector level for both exporting and non-exporting firms.

This pattern is supported by Mann-Whitney U test which determines an insignificant difference between exporting and non-exporting manufacturers in terms of their owners/managers' age (z=score = -0.754 and p-value = 0.451). Exporting and non-exporting firms were found to have relatively equal mean ranks in their owners/managers' age.

Figure 4.9: Manufacturing SMEs by Sub-sector, Export Development and Managerial Age (Frequency Distribution)

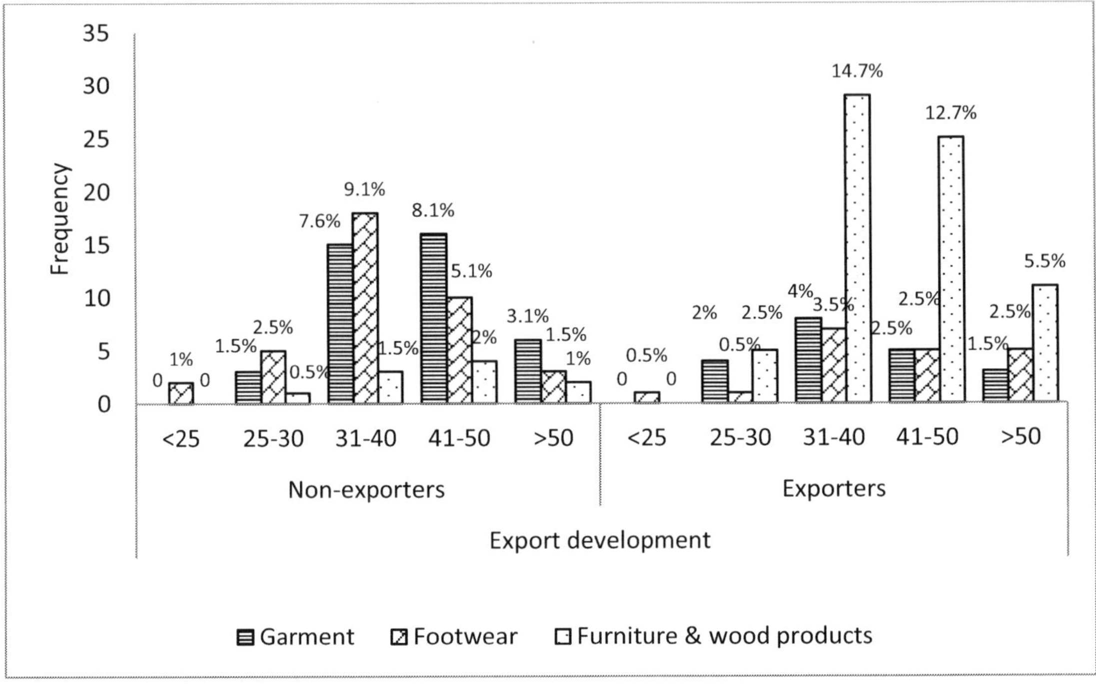

Source: Derived from survey data.

These findings suggest that in the context of Indonesia, the average age of the entrepreneur does not significantly determine their tolerance toward challenges and risks of export endeavours. The results, then, fail to provide support for previous empirical research findings (Leonidou et al. 1998; Ross, 1989; Tseng and Yu; 1991; Ursic and Czinkota, 1989) suggesting the age of the entrepreneur as a determinant of export involvement.

4.3.2 Level of Education

The investigation on the highest level of education achieved by owners/managers is presented in Figure 4.10. These results show that the majority of respondents, despite their level of export development, held a diploma or bachelor degree as their highest level of education (58 per cent). About 12 per cent had achieved

Master and PhD level and the other 30 per cent had only finished elementary or high school for their highest level. Exporters are more prominent than non-exporters at the higher education levels. The findings at sub-sector level show a relatively similar distribution, in that firms of all sub-sectors were most numerous at the diploma and bachelor degree level of education. None of the non-exporters owners/managers from wood products, however, had a Masters or PhD.

The findings from the Mann-Whitney U test support the significant difference between exporters and non-exporters in relation to the owners/managers' education level as z-score = -3.357 and p-value = 0.001. The mean rank of exporters' education (mean rank = 109.80) is found to be significantly higher than that of non-exporters (mean rank = 85.62). Hence, firms with significantly better educated work forces would be likely to have greater commitment to exporting and ability to understand and anticipate foreign markets' settings. These findings are consistent with Berry and Levy's study in Berry and Nugent (1999). They conducted fieldwork in Java among garment, wooden furniture and rattan SMEs exporters and found SMEs exporters to be fairly well educated in comparison with SME entrepreneurs in general.

Figure 4.10: Manufacturing SMEs by Sub-sector, Export Development and Managerial Education (Frequency Distribution)

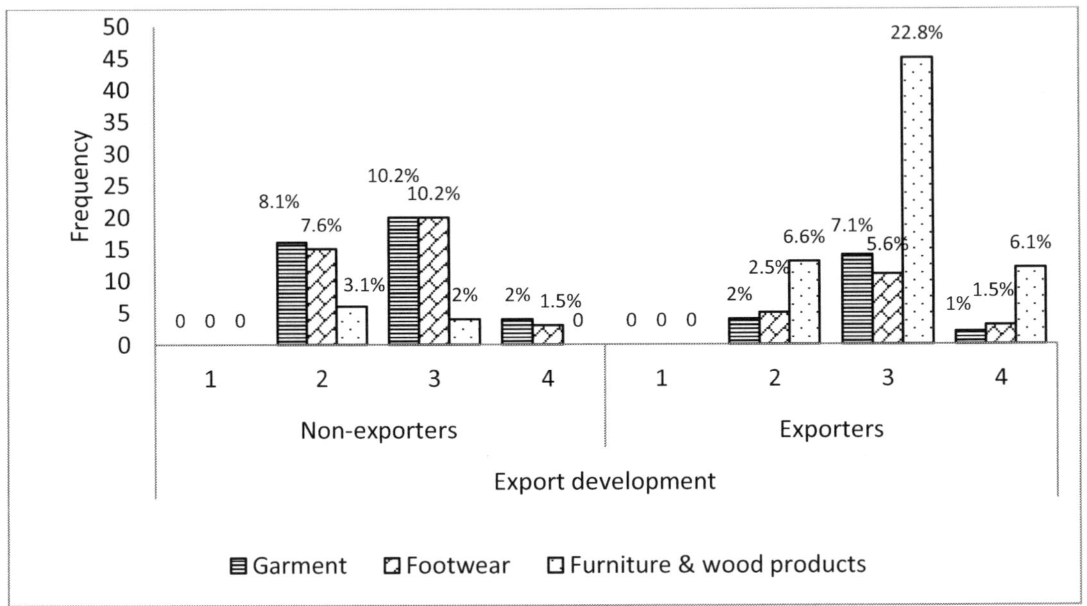

Notes: 1 = owners/managers without education; 2 = owners/managers with elementary and secondary education; 3 = owners/managers with diploma and bachelor education; 4 = owners/managers with master and doctoral education (Suarez-ortega and Alamo-vera's study (2005).

Source: Derived from survey data.

The complexity and accuracy needed in dealing with export documentation and bureaucracy requires managers who are not only well educated but also able to understand the operation and tackle the mechanics of exporting. While the role of education in export planning and performance has been extensively discussed elsewhere (Samiee and Walters, 1999; Axinn, 1988; Reid, 1983; Simpson and Kujawa, 1974; Mayer and Flynn, 1973), the present findings has strengthened the importance of knowledge acquisition in reducing the risk perceived by the individual (Gray, 1997) and thus promoting a more open-minded and interested evaluation of the benefits and disadvantages of exporting (Garnier, 1982).

4.3.3 Experience Abroad

Experience abroad refers to the owners/managers' previous opportunities to live, work or study abroad. Every respondent was asked a series of questions which were not necessarily mutually exclusive, so affirmative responses to one or many of the statements ("I was born overseas"; "my parents were born abroad"; "I have lived/worked abroad for some time"; and "I have received some/all of my education abroad"), were treated as a single affirmative response. The findings reveal that 85 per cent of the sample does not have any previous international exposure (see Figure 4.11).

Figure 4.11: Manufacturing SMEs by Sub-sector, Export Development and Managerial International Experience (Frequency Distribution)

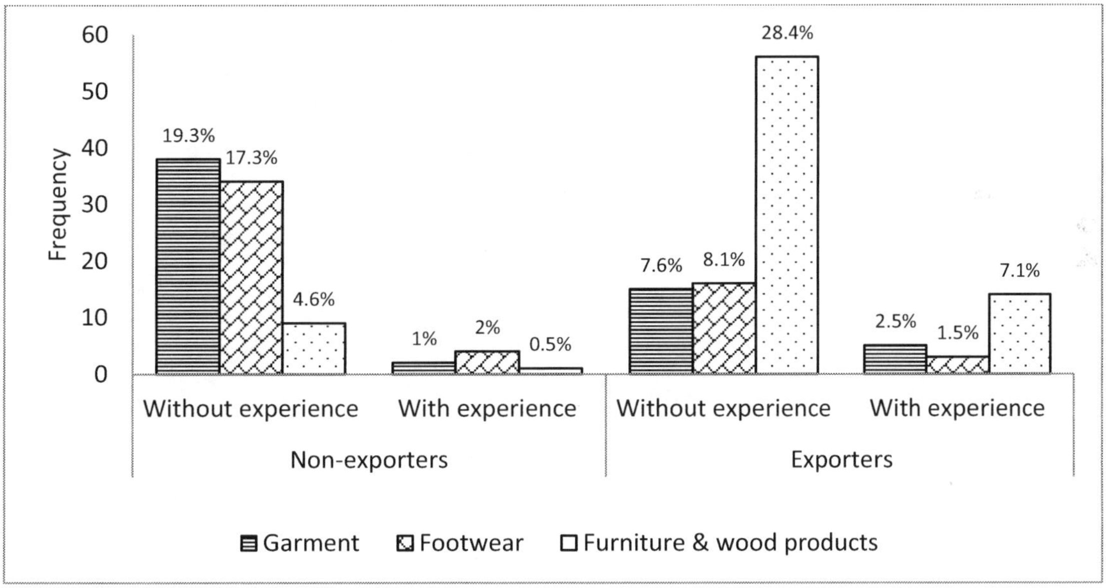

Source: Derived from survey data.

The Mann-Whitney U test was conducted to find out whether there was a significant difference between exporters and non-exporters in their international experience and the results indicate that the mean rank of exporters' international experience (mean rank = 104.38) was significantly higher than that of non-exporters (mean rank = 92.34) at the 5 per cent significance level. The results indicated a z-score of -2.402 and p-value of 0.016.

These results reinforce previous empirical findings suggesting that decision makers of exporting firms are likely to have spent part of their lives abroad (Boatler, 1994; Garnier, 1982). Hence, they are more likely to have the ability to build contacts or networks that can be used to exploit international market opportunities than those who do not own such connections.

4.3.4 Foreign Language Proficiency

The study collected data on the number of foreign languages in which the owners of the firms were proficient. Most of the owners or 62.5 percent of the sample indicated that they were proficient in at least one foreign language, being English which is the common business language of Indonesia. Along with English, 2 per cent of respondents indicated that they were proficient in Italian, 4 per cent in German, and 3.5 per cent in each of French and Dutch.

The results in Figure 4.12 show that the majority of respondents (42 per cent) indicate they have a fair level of proficiency in English; 12.5 percent did not know how to speak English at all; and only 6.5 percent report an excellent ability to converse in this language. Generally, exporters demonstrate greater English language proficiency, that is fair to excellent, than do non-exporters. as the proficiency level advances from a fair to an excellent level.

Figure 4.12: Manufacturing SMEs by Sub-sector, Export Development and Managerial English Language Proficiency (Frequency Distribution)

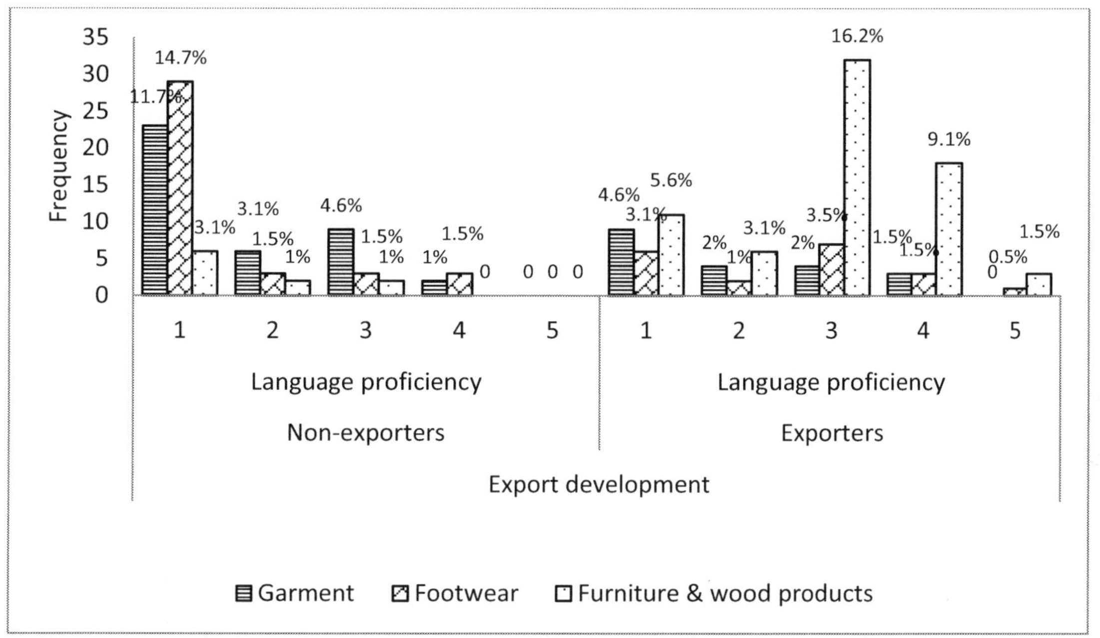

Notes: 1 = not proficient at all; 2 = poorly proficient; 3 = fairly proficient; 4 = good proficiency in English; excellent proficiency in English (Suarez-ortega and Alamo-vera's study (2005).

Source: Derived from survey data.

The Mann-Whitney U test results suggest that exporting managers speak significantly better English than their non-exporting counterparts (z-score = -4.544, p-value = 0.000). The mean rank of exporters' proficiency level (mean rank = 114.80) was higher than that of non-exporters (79.43). These significant results imply a positive link between the language skills of the manager and the firm's export development level. Pertaining to the data, foreign language proficiency is not only useful in securing business transactions, but it is also helpful in improving managers' cultural understanding of overseas markets. The communication breakdown identified in about a quarter of the total respondents could lead to a failure to adapt to individual foreign markets' specifications and requirements.

4.4 Export Characteristics of Manufacturing SMEs in Indonesia

The methodological chapter sets out the manner in which the level of export development was to be specified. The stage of export development was measured by five situation statements and then validated by several proxy measures which include: (a) proportion of sales exported or export intensity; (b) propensity to export or to expand export operation in the near future.

4.4.1 Export Development - In the first classification, the respondents were asked to choose among five possible states of export development that best described their company with respect to export activity. These self-clustering options are as follows: (1) Your firm has never exported and has no intention to do so in the near future;(2) Your firm has never exported but it interested in starting to export; (3) Your firm has marginally exported, but the experience has been somewhat disappointing;(4) Your firm has had profitable export experiences, but is only taking the first step towards international markets; (5) Your firm is an experienced exporter.

According to Figure 4.13, the majority of respondent firms (68 firms or 34.5 per cent) considered themselves in the state 2 group, or interested non-exporters. Fourty nine firms or 24.8 per cent considered themselves as state 5, intensive exporters. While 40 firms or 20.3 per cent see themselves as state 4, non-intensive exporters. Only 9.6 per cent and 10.7 per cent of the respondents considered themselves as the uninterested non-exporters (state 1) and marginal exporters with disappointing experience (state 3) respectively. The findings at sub-sector level reveal that garment and footwear firms mostly congregate in the state 2 situation. Furniture and wood products firms dominate states 4 and 5.

Figure 4.13: Manufacturing SMEs by Sub-sector and Stage of Export Development (Frequency Distribution)

Notes: 1 = 'your firm has never exported and has no intention to do so in the near future'; 2 = 'your firm has never exported but is interested in starting to export'; 3 = 'your firm has exported marginally, but the experience has been somewhat disappointing'; 4 = 'your firm has had profitable export experiences, but is only taking the first steps towards international markets; 5 = 'your firm is an experienced exporter' (Suarez-ortega and Alamo-vera, 2005)

Source: Derived from survey data.

These findings, once more, provide evidence of the higher export development of furniture and wood products compare to those of the garment and footwear industries. Despite, the declining demand in the world market due to the global economic conditions recently, export markets are still considered more profitable opportunity than domestic ones for wood and furniture products.

Export intention is defined as intention to begin/expand exports within the next two years and is designed to distinguish and classify firms in state 3 into exporters or non-exporters; and firms in state 2 into interested or uninterested non-exporter groups.

Figure 4.14: Manufacturing SMEs by Sub-sector and Intention to begin/expand Exports (Frequency Distribution)

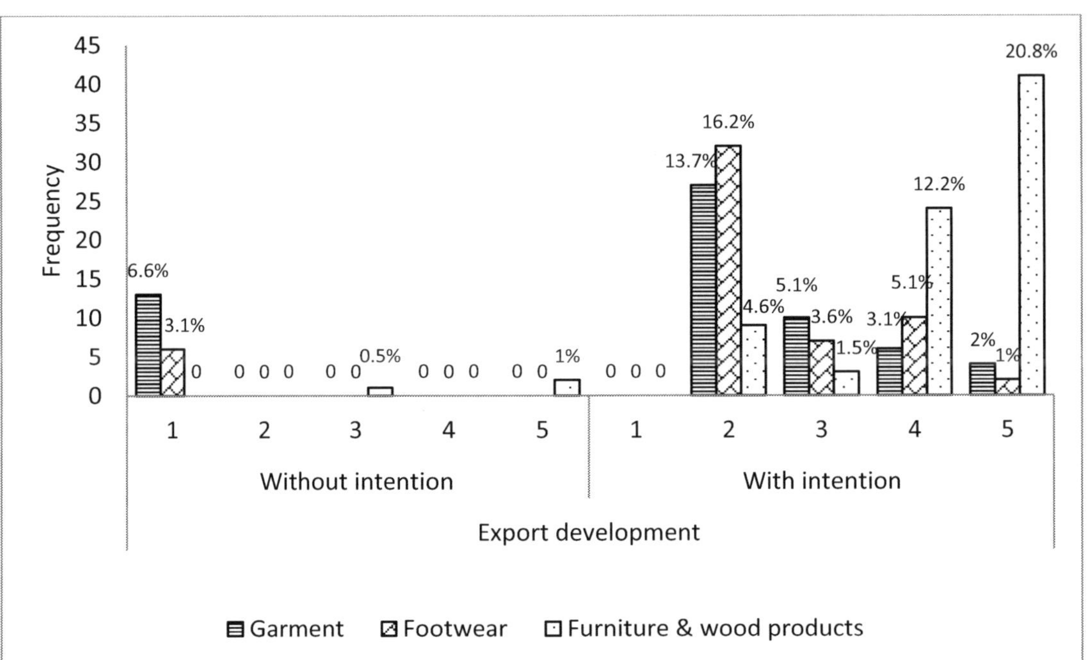

Notes: 1 = 'your firm has never exported and has no intention to do so in the near future'; 2 = 'your firm has never exported but is interested in starting to export'; 3 = 'your firm has exported marginally, but the experience has been somewhat disappointing'; 4 = 'your firm has had profitable export experiences, but is only taking the first steps towards international markets; 5 = 'your firm is an experienced exporter' (Suarez-ortega and Alamo-vera, 2005)

Source: Derived from survey data.

Figure 4.14 reports that nearly all firms (95 per cent) in state 3 indicate that they intend to expand their export operation within the next two years. Hence, although most firms in this state were suspending their export operation due to prior unsatisfactory results, they still have a strong intention to continue exporting in the near future. Likewise all the firms in state 2 express an intention to export in the next two years. Twenty firms, with no intention to export their products, come from the non-exporting garment and footwear sub-sectors.

4.4.2 Export Intensity - An investigation into the percentage of sales exported, or export intensity, is presented in Figure 4.15. The findings reveal that 59 firms, or 30 per cent of the sample, are exporting equal to or more than 50 per cent of their total sales volume. While 37 firms or 18.9 per cent are exporting less than 50 per cent of their total sales volume.

Figure 4.15: Manufacturing SMEs by Sub-sector and Export Intensity (Frequency Distribution)

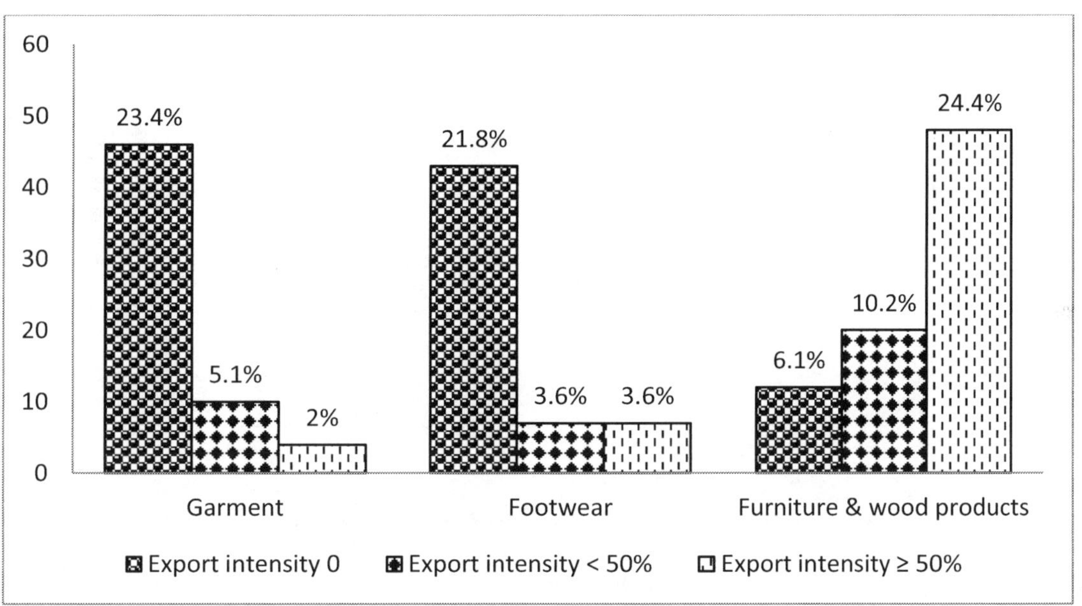

Source: Derived from survey data.

The intensity, at the sub-sector level, shows that about 85 per cent of the 68 firms in furniture and wood products are conducting exporting at some level. On the contrary, about 76 per cent of each of the garment and footwear sub-sectors, or 46 firms in garment and 43 firms in footwear respectively, were not exporting at all.

4.4.3 Export Propensity- The likelihood or the desire for the company to export its product(s) in the next two years is presented in Figure 4.16. The results show that 54.3 per cent of respondents are most likely to export within the next two years. At the other extreme, 21.9 per cent of respondents are most unlikely to export within the next two years. The remaining 23.9 per cent of respondents are still uncertain as to whether or not they will be exporting within the next two years.

Figure 4.16: Manufacturing SMEs by Sub-sector and Export Propensity (Frequency Distribution)

Notes: 1 = 'very unlikely to export in the next two years'; 2 = 'unlikely to export in the next two years'; 3 = 'moderate chance to export in the next two years'; 4 = 'likely to export in the next two years'; 5 = 'very likely to export in the next two years' (Suarez-ortega and Alamo-vera, 2005)

Source: Derived from survey data.

4.5 Chapter Summary

In this chapter, descriptive analysis using crosstab, chi-square test, and independent sample t-test are used to investigate the distribution of the responding firms in relation to their organisational and managerial characteristics. A number of major findings are reported. Among organisational factors proposed in the conceptual framework, only principal and proxy measures of firm size as well as firm age provide significant results in the mean difference between exporting and non-exporting firms. Medium exporting firms are revealed to have a higher mean in full time employees used than that of medium non-exporting firms. The mean difference of full time employees used by small exporting firms as compared to small non-exporting firms was found to be insignificant. Similarly the proxy measure of assets value also shows significant difference between exporters and non-exporters in their mean ranks of this variable. This observation confirms that the mean rank of assets value owned by exporters was found to be significantly higher than that of non-exporters.

Among managerial aspects, education level and foreign language also show significant mean differences based on export development. International business experience was found to have a significant relationship with export development. These significant differences provide preliminary information on how managerial characteristics and organisation of the firm intersect to determine exporting and non-exporting groups of firms. These findings, however, are based on assessment of each variable in isolation of other variables (*ceteris paribus*). This analysis needs to be validated by a further test in which all variables are analysed simultaneously using the path analysis model. The weight of relationships is expected to change as other variables might contribute adversely to the existing individual results.

In regards to the classification of exporting activities, it is found that the majority of firms are in the interested non-exporters (state 2) and initial exporters (state 4) groups with garment and footwear producers dominating the first group. Furniture and wood producers stand out in states 4 and 5. Two variables, export intensity and export propensity, are used as proxy measures for export development. The results generated from these three proxies show a relatively similar distribution and therefore provide validity to the level of export development.

The findings in this Chapter 4 have highlighted firm size, firm age, managerial education level, managerial experience abroad, and managerial language proficiency as key factors in export development of Indonesian SMEs. The significant difference between exporting and non-exporting firms in each of these factors, have provided a partial support to the idea that the performance of an organisation is a result of a continuous interaction with other groups of variables (Cavusgil and Nevin, 1981; Madsen, 1987; Zou and Stan, 1998; Ibeh and Young, 2001; Suarez-ortega and Alamo-vera, 2005), namely its own organisational and managerial characteristics. Several limitations of previous studies such as lack of interaction effects, the question of causality, and the exclusion of external determinants in previous studies (Madsen, 1987) will be aimed to be addressed Chapters 5 in order to provide full support to the findings in Chapter 4. The findings in Chapter 4 were based on an individual analysis by using univariate techniques which needed to be validated by a further test in which all variables were analyzed simultaneously in the path analysis and measured for their regression weights on export development variable and its proxies.

****

CHAPTER FIVE

EMPIRICAL ANALYSIS OF THE CAUSAL RELATIONSHIPS: ORGANISATIONAL AND MANAGERIAL CHARACTERISTICS AND EXPORT DEVELOPMENT

5.1 Introduction

This chapter will combine and measure all organisational and managerial factors concurrently in path analysis and measure for their regression weights on the export development, export propensity, and export intensity variables. The weight of relationships is expected to change according to the extent to which the inclusion of other variables contributes adversely to the existing individual results.

In this analysis, the causal relationships between criterion and predictor variables, developed in the conceptual framework, is performed in an attempt to test hypotheses 1 to 8. The structural model, with predictor variables equivalent to firm size, firm age, education level, and foreign language will be analysed to evaluate their relationships with export development, export propensity, and export intensity. A conventional path analysis in AMOS was used to examine this relationship. Path analysis has the ability to incorporate latent and measured constructs into the analysis (Cunningham, 2007; Hair et al., 1998). Path analysis has been used to study consumer behaviour, psychology, and management. Hair et al. (1998) maintained that path analysis provides a simple way of dealing simultaneously with multiple relationships and is capable of assessing these relationships.

The organisation of the chapter is as follows: Section 5.2 examines the magnitude of organisational and managerial characteristics affecting export development. Section 5.3 presents an analysis on organisational and managerial characteristics affecting export propensity. Section 5.4 investigates the magnitude of organisational and managerial characteristics influencing export intensity. Section 5.5 summarizes the key findings of the chapter.

5.2 Organisational and managerial factors of the firm and export development

Path analysis is an approach that extends regression analysis by providing a way of testing the adequacy of a model through examination of the differences or residuals between the sample and model implied correlations (Asher, 1983). A regression is done for each variable in the model as a dependent or criterion on others which the model indicates as causes or predictors. The regression weights predicted by the path model are then compared with the observed correlation matrix for the variables, and a goodness-of-fit statistic is calculated (Cunningham, 2007). Path analysis, in addition, requires the usual assumptions of regression. In Chapter 5 the following hypotheses were tested individually by using crosstab or standard t-test. In this second stage of analysis, all criterion variables in each hypothesis were regressed simultaneously to quantify their relationships with export development, export propensity, and export intensity.

H1: Manager's age is perceived to have a negative effect on the level of export development, thus having a negative effect on export propensity and intensity.

H2: Manager's educational level is perceived to have a positive effect on the level of export development, thus having a positive effect on export propensity and intensity.

H3: Manager's experience abroad is perceived to have a positive effect on the level of export development, thus having a positive effect on export propensity and intensity

H4: Manager's foreign language proficiency is perceived to have a positive effect on the level of export development, thus having a positive effect on export propensity and intensity.

H5: Firm's size has a positive effect on export development and export propensity, but a negative effect on export intensity.

H6: Firm's age is perceived to have a negative effect on export development, export propensity and intensity.

H7: Firm's geographic market development is perceived to have a positive effect on export development, export propensity and intensity.

H8: Firm's location is perceived to have a negative effect on the level of export development, thus having a negative effect on export propensity and intensity.

The initial path model was not a good fit to the data at 5 per cent significance level as $\chi^2(503) = 726.633, \rho = 0.000$. The results indicate a consistent misspecification between export development and export intensity as well as between export development and export propensity. The model is re-specified by including the direct path from export development to export intensity and from export development to export propensity. The paths imply that export development functions as a proxy that can help explain the level of export intensity and export propensity. All paths that have standardized residual covariance larger than 2 in absolute value were extracted to improve the model fitness.

The adjusted model is presented in Figure 5.1. In general, large standardized residuals overall are indicative of a poorly fitting model. As maintained by Cunningham (2007), examining the standardized residuals is the most reliable method of identifying the source of model misspecification. When the structural and measurement models are estimated, the standardised regression weight or standardised loading coefficients provide an estimate of the reliabilities of the indicators and the overall constructs. The model in this study consisted of multiple paths into export development, export propensity, and export intensity, being the three endogenous or criterion variables.

After extracting the paths with large standardized residuals and low reliabilities as well as adding direct paths from export development to export intensity and export propensity, the model fits the data well, $\chi^2(427) = 463.053$, $\rho = 0.111$. The goodness of fit indices for the adjusted model are presented in Table 6.1. The interpretation of these indices is informed by SME literature (see for example: Schumacker and Lomax, 1996; Hu and Bentler, 1998; Hutchinson and Olmos, 1998).

Figure 5.1: Model Re-specification of Organisational and Managerial Factors Affecting Export Development, Export Propensity, and Export Intensity

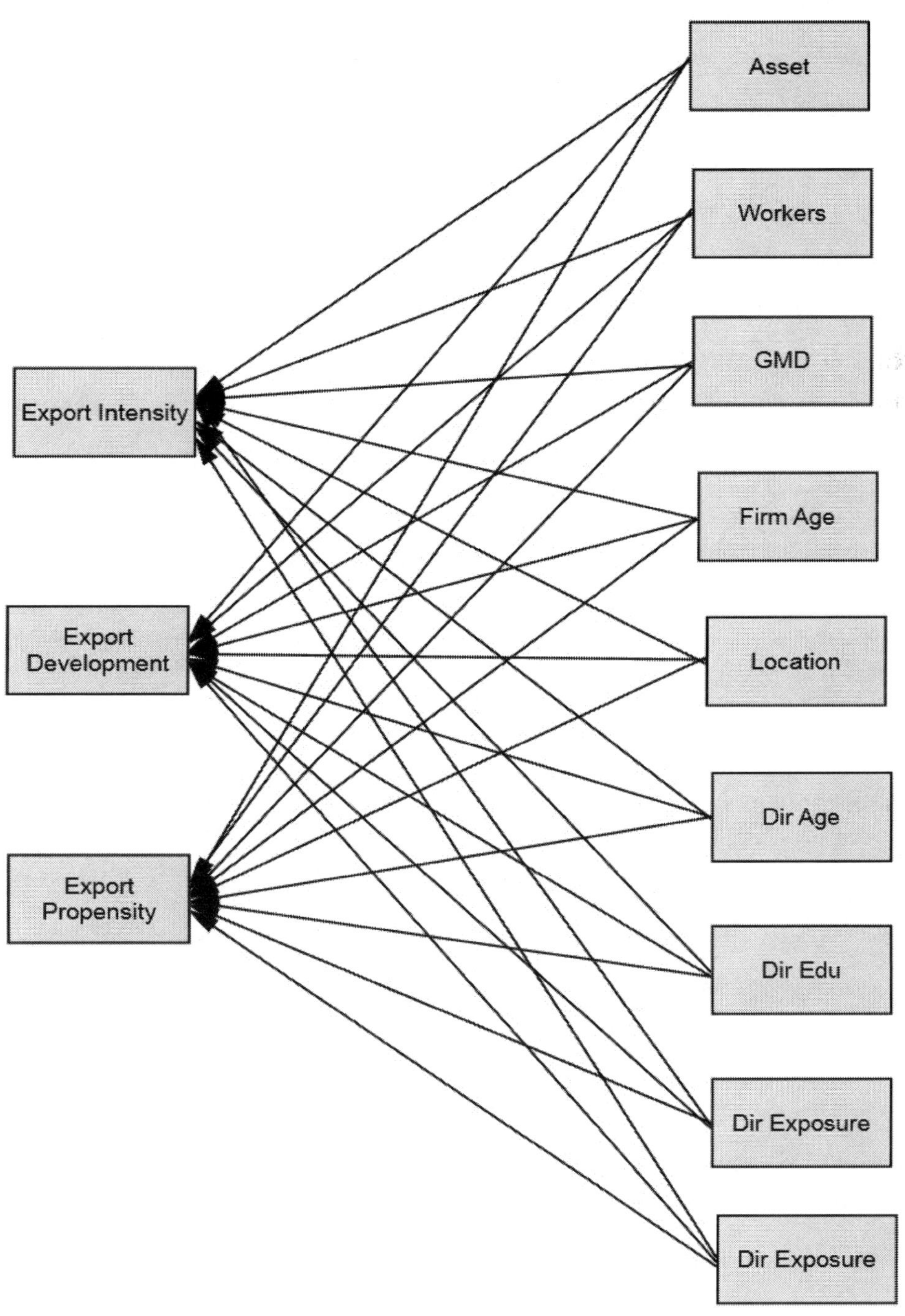

Source: Derived from survey data.

All indices, in general, indicate that the model provides an adequate fit to data. Of the seven model-fit measures, AGFI and NFI were slightly below the required level of 0.90 but they still suggest a reasonable model fit (Hu and Bentler, 1998). Once the overall model fit was confirmed, focus moved to the testing of hypotheses. Maximum likelihood estimation is adopted. This estimate is obtained by means of an iterative procedure that minimizes a definite fitting function by successively improving the parameter estimates starting with the initial estimates (Joreskog and Sorbom, 1982).

The hypotheses were tested by determining the statistical significance of the path coefficients. To evaluate the estimated causal relations, the actual size of each parameter was assessed in terms of the standardized β coefficients and ρ-values. In order to ease the analysis, the regression weights for managerial and organisational factors in predicting each of export development, export propensity, and export intensity are presented in separate figures and tables. The following Table 5.2 present the regression weights for managerial and organisational factors in predicting export development. While the regression weights for managerial and organisational factors in predicting export propensity can be found in Appendix 1 and for export intensity in Appendix 2. In the discussion that follows the results by export development, export intensity and export propensity will be covered contiguously.

Table 5.1: Model Fit Indices of Factors Affecting Export Development

	Overall model fit							
Measurement model	**Model fit**					**Model comparison**		
Model fit indices	CMIN/DF[1]	SRMR[2]	RMSEA[3]	GFI[4]	AGFI[4]	NFI[5]	TLI[6]	CFI[7]
Level of acceptable model fit	<2	<.05	<0.08	>0.90	>0.90	>0.90	>0.90	>0.90
Factors Affecting Export Development	1.084	0.0314	0.021	0.906	0.810	0.895	0.981	0.990

Notes:1) CMIN/DF is the minimum discrepancy divided by its degrees of freedom. Suggested ratios in the range of 2 to 1 or 3 to 1 (Wheaton et al., 1977; Carmines and McIver, 1981; Marsh and Hocevar, 1985)

2) SRMR is the average difference between corresponding elements of the sample and the model-implied correlations matrices. A model is fit when SRMR is less than 0.05 (Hu and Bentler, 1999);

3) RMSEA is a fit index that uses the confidence interval to indicate the precision of the estimate of fit. RMSEA value should be about 0.05 or less (Browne and Cudeck in Bollen and Long, 1993)

4) GFI/AGFI give an indication of the relative amounts of the covariances among the latent variables that are accounted for by the model and it should be between 0 and 1. The value exceeding 0.90 is preferred (Mathieu et al., 1992);

5) NFI calculates the minimum discrepancy of the model and the value should be less than 0.90 (Bentler and Bonett, 1980);

6) TLI estimates the relative improvement per degree of freedom of the target model over an independence model and the value should be exceeding 0.95 (Hu and Bentler, 1998);

7) CFI measures the improvement of a target model and an independence model. Its value should be greater than 0.95 (Hu and Bentler, 1999).

Source: Derived from survey data.

The results establish that the relationships between the three dependent variables and each of the managerial and organisational factors is weakly linear. The sample correlations range from a low of .009 to a high of .430. Firstly, it is noted that number of employees and value of assets as measures of firm size are positively correlated with the level of export development, export propensity, and export intensity. The correlation coefficients for the number of employees range between 0.171 and 0.271, indicating it has very weak positive relationships with export development and its proxies. The correlation coefficient on value of assets with the export development variable and its proxies shows slightly stronger positive linear relationships.

Despite its weak correlation, the regression weight for the number of employees in the prediction of export development is found significantly different from zero at the 0.05 level. Amount of assets is found to be significant in predicting export development, export propensity and export intensity of the firm at the 0.05 level. It is estimated that for every additional unit increase in the number of employees, export development would rise by 0.131. While with every unit increase in the amount of assets, export development, export propensity, and export intensity would rise by 0.161, 0.126, and 0.096 respectively (see βeta weights column in Table 5.2, Appendix 1 and Appendix 2). Hence, H6 (firm's size has a positive effect on export development and export propensity, but a negative effect on export intensity) is partially accepted at the 5 per cent significance level as the amount of assets has positive effects not only on export development and export propensity but also on export intensity.

Thirdly, the firm age variable also displays a very weak correlation with export development and its proxies. The coefficients range between 0.090 and 0.177. Regardless of its weak correlation, firm age is found to be significantly different from zero at the 0.10 significance level in predicting export development and export intensity. Based on these findings, H6 (Firm's age has a positive effect on the level of export development and on export propensity and intensity) is accepted at the 0.10 significance level for showing positive effects on export development and export intensity.

Fourthly, a weak correlation was also noticed between geographic market development (GMD) and the level of export development. The correlations between GMD and export development and its proxies range from 0.133 to 0.166. Consonant with its low correlations coefficient, the regression weight of this item shows an insignificant result in predicting the level of export development, export propensity, and export intensity. H7 (Firm's geographic market development has a positive effect on the level of export development, thus having positive effect on export propensity and intensity), consequently, is rejected at the 5 per cent significance level for not influencing export development or its proxies.

Table 5.2: Managerial and Organisational Determinants of Export Development

	r^b	Unstandardized Coefficients B	Unstandardized Coefficients S.E.[c]	Standardized Coefficients βeta	t	Sig.
Export devt ← Amount of assets	0.398	0.293	0.103	0.161	2.855	***
Export devt ← Number of workers	0.271	0.001	0.000	0.131	2.485	**
Export devt ← Geographic market devt	0.138	0.061	0.038	0.078	1.597	NS
Export devt ← Firm age	0.177	0.013	0.007	0.101	1.914	*
Export devt ← Location	-0.023	-0.090	0.103	-0.044	-0.867	NS
Export devt ← Director's age	0.137	0.037	0.057	0.035	0.655	NS
Export devt ← Director's education	0.253	0.101	0.093	0.064	1.077	NS
Export devt ← Director's experience abroad	0.209	-0.017	0.151	-0.006	-0.116	NS
Export devt ← Director's language profic.	0.429	0.207	0.056	0.221	3.696	****

Notes: a) Export development; b) r = correlation coefficient; c) S.E. = Standard error; d) NS = Not significant; * $\rho < 0.10$; ** $\rho < 0.05$; *** $\rho < 0.01$; **** $\rho < 0.001$

Source: Derived from survey data.

Fifthly, the findings show an almost negligible negative relationship between location and export development and its proxies. The coefficients range from as low as -0.005 to -0.193. The regression weight on location is also found to be significant in predicting the propensity of the firm to export at the 0.05 level. Hence, if location should increase by a unit, export propensity is expected to fall by 0.126 units (see Appendix 1). This, however, was irrelevant for the other two criterion variables in which t-values were insignificant. H8 (Firm's location has a negative effect on the level of export development and thus on export propensity and intensity) therefore, is partially accepted at the 5 per cent significance level for not influencing export development and export intensity.

In relation to manager's or director's age, the correlation coefficients indicate that it has a weak positive correlation with the level of export development and export intensity (0.137 and 0.124 respectively) and a very weak negative correlation with the firm's propensity to export (-0.016). The regression weight of age was found to be significant in predicting the level of export propensity at the 0.10 significance level. When other predictor variables in the model are controlled, export propensity would increase by 0.106 unit for every unit decrease in manager's or director's age. H1 (Manager's age has a negative effect on the level of export development and on export propensity and intensity), therefore, is partially accepted for not influencing the level of export development and export intensity

Manager's or director's educational level additionally shows weakly positive correlations with the level of export development, export propensity, and export intensity. The regression weight of educational level is insignificant in predicting the level of export development, export propensity and export intensity (see Table 5.2 and Appendices 1 and 2). Hence, H2 (Manager's educational level has a positive effect on level of export development and on export propensity and intensity). is rejected for the variable showing no effects on export development and its proxies.

Likewise, managerial experience abroad is weakly positively correlated with the level of export development and its proxies. The weak correlation ranged from 0.092 to 0.209. Consistent with the weak correlation, the regression weights of experience abroad are insignificant in predicting the level of export development as well as its proxies at the 5 per cent significance level (see Table 5.2, Appendices 1 and 2). H3 (Managerial experience abroad has a positive effect on the level of export development and on export propensity and intensity) as a result, is rejected for not affecting export development and its proxies.

Manager's or director's language proficiency, in addition, is found to have a weak positive correlation with the level of export development, export propensity, and export intensity. The correlation coefficients range from as low as .238 to as high as .429. The regression weights of language proficiency are significant in predicting the level of export development and export intensity, but not significant enough in predicting export propensity. It is expected that there will be an increase by 0.221 and 0.086 in the level of export development and export intensity respectively when foreign language proficiency increases by a unit (see Table 5.2, Appendices 1 and 2). H4 (Manager's foreign language proficiency is perceived to have a positive effect on the level of export development and on export propensity and intensity) as a consequence, is partially accepted for not influencing export propensity. The summary of the hypotheses' testings and their subsequent results are presented in Table 5.3.

Table 5.3: Results of Model Testing

Hypotheses (Correlation and Causality)		**ρ**	**Results Causality**
Firm size → Export development & proxies	H10	0.05	Partially accepted
Distinctive capabilities →Export development & proxies	H9	0.10	Partially accepted
Firm age → Export development & proxies	H11	0.10	Partially accepted
GMD → Export development & proxies	H12	0.05	Rejected
Location → Export development & proxies	H13	0.05	Partially accepted
Age → Export development & proxies	H1	0.10	Partially accepted
Education → Export development & proxies	H2	0.05	Rejected
Experience abroad →Export development & proxies	H3	0.05	Rejected
Foreign language → Export development & proxies	H4	0.05	Partially accepted

Source: Derived from survey data.

5.3 Chapter Summary

To summarize, investigations using path analysis have developed a full model of multiple regressions which examined the relationships between dependent or criterion variables, and a number of independent or predictor variables. Criterion variables that were tested individually in previous chapters using crosstab, chi-square, and the standard t-test, were regressed simultaneously onto all criterion or endogenous variables in one structural model.

The first saturated model for all possible paths and correlations revealed large differences or residuals between the sample and model implied correlations. The significant χ^2 statistic was used to justify the model unfitness. Additional paths from export development to export intensity and from export development to export propensity and removal of paths with a standardized residual covariance (larger than 2 in absolute value) improved the model fitness.

All model fit indices, suggested a general fit of the model. The relationship between the level of export development and each of the managerial organisational factors, in general, was weakly positively linear. The findings on the regression weights, to some extent supported these weak correlations with the exception of the factors: number of employees; the amount of assets; distinctive capabilities; firm location; manager's or director's age; and manager's or director's language proficiency. Every additional unit increase in each of these significant factors increased export development and/or its proxies by the magnitude reported in the text above.

****

CHAPTER SIX

SUMMARY, CONCLUSIONS AND IMPLICATIONS OF THE FINDINGS

6.1 Policy Background, Research Objectives and Industry Review

The purpose of this research was to undertake an empirical study to investigate the particular organizational and managerial determinants of the different aspects of a firm's export development process of manufacturing SMEs in Indonesia.

The specific objectives of the study were:

1) To investigate the relational differences between managerial and organisational factors and the level of export development of manufacturing exporters and non-exporters in Indonesia.
2) To make policy recommendations for promoting manufacturing SMEs' exports from Indonesia.

The present study has synthesized and integrated aspects from each of the existing determinants of export behaviour models, including managerial characteristics, organisational characteristics, export development, export propensity, and export intensity into the conceptual framework. The study employed a quantitative approach using multivariate data analysis.

The study, based on personally administered questionnaires on 197 SMEs owners or managers, identified that the export development of Indonesian manufacturing SMEs is explained by interrelated factors of firm size, firm location, managerial age, and foreign language ability. These findings contribute to a better understanding of the export development process of SMEs in a developing country context.

Three sub-sectors, namely textiles; garments, leather and footwear; and furniture and wood products, were selected for analysis because the sub-sectors contain a concentration of SMEs as the main players. The structure and performance of the sub-sectors over the last two decades was reviewed. Textile, garment and footwear industries began to grow in the 1970s and garments and footwear were significant exports from Indonesia in the 1980s. The number of establishments in these two sub-sectors, however, has decreased in the last two decades.

The garment and footwear sub-sectors were mainly controlled by domestic private producers, being around 90 per cent of all producers. Most firms from these two sub-sectors were situated in Java and locations in the Sumatera islands. The textile, garment, and footwear industries are major contributors to non-oil manufacturing GDP and export earnings in Indonesia; more than 50 per cent of SMEs' exports come from these three sub-sectors (Sandee and Ibrahim, 2002; Basri and van der Eng, 2004). The sub-sectors also accounted for substantial investment formation in the economy.

Furniture and wood products manufacturing was another sub-sector of interest. This industry has been growing rapidly since the Indonesian government imposed a ban on log exports and restrictions on processed wood exports in 1990. To compensate for plummeting domestic purchasing power in the 1997 Asian crisis, the industry increased its profits through export. The government through its foreign and domestic scheme directed this industry to focus on high added value finished products to increase the industry's revenue.

The total number of establishment of furniture and wood products in Indonesia also declined in the last two decades. Like the previous two sub-sectors, ownership here is dominated by the domestic, private producers. The majority of the producers are concentrated in Java with furniture firms generally located in Central Java, Yogyakarta, and West Java provinces, while wood producers tend to be spread around Java and Bali. The majority of firms in this sub-sector are serving overseas markets. Their share of total non-oil exports, however, has been growing gradually since the Asian financial crisis.

Despite unfavourable global conditions, Indonesian SMEs still aspire to seize export opportunity and develop in terms of output and employment growth. Government policy seeks to promote an efficient and dynamic SME sector and create an environment which allows them to grow without long-term dependence on government support (Berry et al., 2001). The export response of SMEs during the crisis corroborates their potential and demonstrates that being less reliant on government support was an additional incentive to grow.

The remaining discussion in this chapter is organized around the four objectives stated earlier. The emphasis will be on drawing conclusions and outlining managerial and public policy implications. The study's contribution to the export literature, its limitations and suggestions for future research are scrutinized in the last two sections.

6.2 A Review of the Research Findings

6.2.1 The development of a conceptual framework for explaining export behaviour of manufacturing SMEs in Indonesia

The literature review in Chapter 2 identified problems and knowledge gaps that establish the need for further examination of manufacturing SMEs' behaviour in Indonesia. As already noted, further studies of Indonesian manufacturing SMEs' export behaviour were inadequate, that is they lacked an empirical model that facilitated understanding and offered a confirmation of critical variables affecting Indonesian SMEs' export development in overseas markets. Evidence supporting this contention is found in the fact that, although the stream of research on export behaviour is growing, both the focus and actuality of the literature still calls for an overview in a developing country context. The recent empirical studies reviewed in Suarez-Ortega and Alamo-Vera (2005) reveal that export behaviour studies carried out in developing countries were almost non-existent. Furthermore, most studies focused on the managerial characteristics and direct effects without trying to bring them together into a framework where the relationships and interactions between the variables could be observed. Hence, there is a need for a new approach to incorporate the most common factors of firm and managerial characteristics to explore their relationship to different stages of the export development process.

Building upon the review of literature, the study uses five categories to investigate the various determinants of export behaviour: managerial characteristics; organisational characteristics; export development; export propensity; and export intensity. Since Indonesia has been pursuing an incremental approach in its economic development policy by initially focusing on import substitution and gradually embracing outward oriented policy, most Indonesian SMEs are assumed to have been following a gradualist approach to enter foreign markets. For measurement purposes, the study follows the generic types of export development stages set out by Leonidou and Katsikeas (1996). The study also uses the proxies of export propensity and export intention to support the export development classification.

The proposed conceptual framework of this study is depicted in Figure 3.1. All predictors belonging to the internal environment of the firm are listed under 'firm characteristics' and 'managerial characteristics'. The correlation between organisational specific resources and management background characteristics and export development determines the firm's level of export development, export propensity, and export intensity. To sum up, the concepts used to develop the proposed framework resemble Suarez-Ortega and Alamo-Vera's (2005) research closely, but this study improves on the older techniques by using a structural equation approach to solve the multidimensional correlations and relationships between each variable in the model.

6.2.2 An assessment of the relational differences between managerial and organisational factors and the level of export development of manufacturing exporters and non-exporters in Indonesia

When the four levels of export development (Leonidou and Katsikeas, 1996), export propensity, and export intensity were denoted as criterion or endogenous variables estimated using managerial and organisational characteristics of a firm as predictor or exogenous variables, the results indicated that the association between the level of export development and each of the managerial and organisational factors was weakly linear.

The number of employees and value of assets, as measures of firm size, were weakly and positively correlated with the level of export development, export propensity, and export intensity. Despite the weak correlations, the regression weight for the number of employees in the prediction of export development was found to be significantly different from zero at the 0.05 level. The amount of assets was also found to be critical in determining the level of export development, export propensity and export intensity of the firm at the 0.05 level. Hence, H5 (Firm's size has a positive effect on the level of export development and on export propensity, but a negative effect on export intensity) is partially accepted at the 5 per cent significance level as although the number of employees has a positive association with export propensity and export intensity, it does not show any positive causal effects on these two proxies of export development. This deduction, to some extent, corroborated previous research findings that the organisation's size is a key determinant of its internationalisation process and the larger the firm, the greater the differential size advantage over smaller firms will be (Katsikeas and Morgan,

1994). Nevertheless, it simultaneously cancelled out the argument that size was not directly correlated with export intensity.

Firm age also produced a very weak correlation with export development and its proxies. Regardless of its weak correlation, firm age was found significantly different from zero at the 0.10 significance level in predicting export development and export intensity. The result indicated that the older the firm, the higher its level of export development and its intensity in export operations. Based on these findings, H6 (Firm's age has a positive effect on the level of export development and on export propensity and intensity) is partially accepted at the 0.10 significance level for showing positive correlations with all criterion variables and positive effects on export development and export intensity.

A weak correlation was also noticed between geographic market development (GMD) and the level of export development. Consonant with its low correlations coefficients, the regression weight of this item showed an insignificant result in predicting the level of export development, export propensity, and export intensity. H7 (Firm's geographic market development has a positive effect on the level of export development and on export propensity and intensity) consequently, is rejected at the 5 per cent significance level for showing a positive association but not influencing export development or its proxies.

The findings reveal an almost negligible negative relationship between location and export development and its proxies. However, in line with the assumption developed in the methodological chapter, geographic proximity of firms to the centres of information and various export stimuli in urban areas does influence propensity toward export operations. The regression weight of location was found significant in predicting the propensity of the firm to export at the 0.05 level. The findings confirmed that in the context of the sample data, the closer the firm's location to the city centre and its business facilities, the more prone it is to export operations. Hence, H8 (Firm's location has a negative effect on the level of export development and on export propensity and intensity) is partially accepted for negatively affecting export propensity at the 0.05 significance level.

In relation to manager's or director's age, the correlation coefficients indicated a weak positive correlation with the level of export development and export intensity and a very weak negative correlation with the firm's propensity to export. The regression weight of manager age was found to be significant in predicting the level of export propensity at the 0.10 significance level. In this case, the younger the manager or the owner, the higher their propensity to export in the next two years. Thus, H1 (Manager's age has a negative effect on the level of export development and on export propensity and intensity) is only partially supported as the observed counts of age were expected to be negatively correlated with the level of export development and export intensity.

Manager's or director's educational level additionally showed weakly positive correlations with the level of export development, export propensity, and export intensity. Consonant with these weak relationships, the regression weights of educational level were found to be insignificant in predicting the level of export development, export propensity, and export intensity. Hence, H2 (Manager's educational level has a positive effect on the level of export development and on export propensity and intensity) is partially accepted as the variable shows a positivc association but no effects on export development and its proxies.

Furthermore, managerial experience abroad was weakly positively correlated with the level of export development and its proxies. Its regression weights were found insignificant in predicting the level of export development as well as its proxies at the 5 per cent significance level.

Manager's or director's language proficiency displayed a weak positive correlation with the level of export development, export propensity, and export intensity. Its regression weights were significant in predicting the level of export development and export intensity, but not significant enough in predicting export propensity. In other words, the more proficient the manager or the owner of the firm is in foreign language, the higher the level of export development and the propensity to export within the next two years. Consequently, H4 (Manager's foreign language proficiency has a positive effect on the level of export development and on export propensity and intensity) is not rejected at the 0.05 significance level as the observed data of language proficiency is approximately similar to the expected hypotheses.

6.2.3 Policy Implications of the Findings

This section presents the implication of the findings and in so doing addresses the study's last objective of providing recommendations for promoting the export endeavour of SMEs in Indonesia. Several implications both for the management decision maker and the public policy maker in their tasks to promote export activity within their respective spheres of influence are raised for discussion.

6.2.3.1 Managerial Policy Implications of the Findings

Managerially, the study provides SME managers with the information to recognize managerial and organisational determinants affecting their level of export development.

The importance of specific characteristics of owner-managers as part of the export decision mechanism in a firm is once again indicated in the final model in which managerial age and foreign language proficiency are significant in explaining export propensity and the level of export development respectively. These two factors, therefore, need special attention. A number of commonly held notions of older owner-managers such as resistance to change, cautiousness and slowness of judgment (Crick and Chaudry, 1996) may exist in the Indonesian context. Thus, the younger the owner-manager's age, the more open-minded and cosmopolitan they are relative to their older counterparts (Leonidou et al., 1998).

Foreign language proficiency is found significant in determining the level of export development and should be acted upon positively by SME owner-managers. Investing in English or other foreign language courses or training would lead to a number of financial, marketing, and other benefits over time as implied earlier in the literature review (Burton and Schlegelmilch's, 1987; Dichtl et al., 1990; Holzmuller and Kasper, 1991; and Leonidou et al., 1998). Owner-managers are required to meet this necessity by willingly and persistently learning foreign language(s) in order to improve their business performance.

The indication from amount of assets, geographic market development, and firm location is that owner-managers need to pay attention to the firm's capacity and competitiveness as priorities that can promote export development. Owner-managers need to be aware that by strengthening their institutional performance to access capital sources, such as banks and other financial institutions, and by developing quality improvement schemes such as training or workshops, they can increase their potential in the international markets.

SMEs' access to both investment and working capital has to be simplified and made affordable. Non-bank financial institutions that perform as alternative capital sources for SMEs need to strengthen their institutional competence and service quality.

Government needs to increase private sector and/or community involvement in providing information technology services and managerial consultancies for SMEs through incentive and establishment supports. By increasing the competition, the cost of acquiring these services is expected to level off to favour SMEs as end users.

It is also suggested that government agencies develop market intelligence systems to understand opportunities and demand challenges for SMEs' products and put them into a suitable market segment based on their product distinctiveness. Improvements in the quality and accessibility of information gathered through market intelligence will, in turn, solve managerial and organisational constrains which were indicated by most non-exporting firms as costly to develop under their own budget.

In regards to the promotion of exports particularly for exporting firms, government-funded programs need to focus on long-term targets. Government agencies need to ensure that SME producers are not only able to win export orders but also maintain their continuous long-term access to export markets by providing managerial and technical assistance in relation to their quality control, consistency in production volumes and products' time delivery. Most non-exporting SMEs indicated a hesitancy to attend a trade show due to cost-benefit considerations. Government agencies, therefore, need to provide subsidies, particularly for 'new comers' who would like to participate in a domestic trade-exhibition or other export promotion program for the first time. In addition, eligibility criteria for support of SME trade fair participation should be improved to ensure fair and equal sponsorships.

Although the programs run by DGNED are relatively well rated by SMEs that have participated in the promotional activities, there is no attempt from national and local (cluster based) associations to combine their export promotion programs. A concerted effort might actually enhance outreach, effectiveness, and sustainability of public interventions. Such a synergy would also encourage networking among firms, support joint marketing efforts, and be beneficial for the development of supporting industries.

Some respondents, during the data collection, commented on the importance of integrating all business aspects including market intelligence, R&D, export finance, infrastructure, human resources, and standardisation and certification policies under one-roof as it can be more cost effective and cost efficient for SMEs as the service users. Current export promotion policies within public agencies (Directorate General of National Export Development (DGNED), Ministry of Cooperatives and SMEs, Indonesian Investment Board, and Tourism Promotion Board), and between public and private sectors lack coordination and often lead to overlapping programs and waste of funding. A closer integration, therefore, not only can facilitate interaction between agencies but also reduce overlap in promotion activities.

6.3 Major Contributions of the Current Study

This research has made a number of contributions to the field of export business theory and practice. These are:

The validation of export business theory, that has previously been tested in a developed country context, for a developing country's business environment via application to a sample of 197 manufacturing SMEs in Indonesia. The differences that exist between developed and developing countries make the findings significant by extending the scope of the theory and then confirming the previous results in a cross sectional research design.

The adoption of path analysis using the AMOS platform made it possible to simultaneously examine the relationships between various managerial and organisational factors and export development in a single model and to quantify these relationships. The study has tested a number of particular hypotheses using multivariate data analysis where previously hypotheses were tested by ignoring interactions and using only univariate data analysis.

The innovation of combining export development, export propensity, and export intensity as predictor or endogenous variables in the conceptual framework. Conceptual models from previous studies were criticized for the unbalanced treatment given to the examination of different export development stages and for ignoring export propensity and export intensity as well as the failure to test concurrently the full set of managerial and organisational factors against the full range of export dimensions (Leonidou, 1998; Suarez-Ortega and Alamo-Vera, 2005).

6.4 Limitations of the Study

Some possible limitations that must be recognized before generalizing the findings to other context are:

- The cross sectional research design involves the collection of data at a single point in time. Such an approach produces the difficulty of detecting respondent's patterns over time, as they might change due to new circumstances emerging.

- The sampling frame of this study is small and medium sized firms dealing in exportable products in three types of sub-sectors that were textiles, garments, footwear, and furniture and wood products. As maintained earlier, the main reason for selecting these industries is because of their concentration of small and medium sized firms involved in exporting from Indonesia (Berry et al. 2001). Thus, although the purpose of this study was to generally understand export behaviour of small and medium sized firms, irrespective of their type of industry, caution should be exercised in any attempt to generalize the findings due to differences at industry and country levels.

6.5 Suggestions for Future Research

- A qualitative approach based on indepth interviews with SME owners or senior managers is needed to confirm their views on all identified factors affecting SMEs export development in this study. By expanding the study to a longitudinal and qualitative research design, insight into dynamic processes could also be gained. Multiple case study methodology would be appropriate to investigate and chart the impact of internal factors on decision making within the firms and the consequent interaction with the level of export development.
- Given the volatile global economy and policy reforms in Indonesia, constant monitoring of these changes and their impact on export development and performance is pertinent.

BIOGRAPHICAL NOTES:

Rita R. Pidani is the Coordinator of Under-graduate Business Program and Lecturer at the UON Singapore which is a wholly-owned entity of the University of Newcastle, Australia. She received her PhD in Economics from the University of Newcastle, Australia. Currently, she is a Lecturer of Business and Commerce Programs and is conducting research activities in the areas of small and medium-sized enterprise development, women's enterprise development, local economic development, and business and financial models for developing countries. She is affiliated with the centre of full employment and equity (cofFEE) at the University of Newcastle.

Frank W. Agbola is the Deputy Head of Newcastle Business School. Dr Agbola has a strong background in applied econometrics, development economics and agricultural economics and has published in several top-tier refereed journals. Dr Agbola has served as a reviewer for a number of ranked-journals such as Urban Studies, Economic Modelling, Applied Economics, Journal of Development Studies, Journal of Rural Studies, Emerging MArkets Finance and Trade, International Journal of Finance and Economics, Annals of Tourism Research, Contemporary Economic Policy, The International Trade Journal, Journal of Economic Policy, Journal of Social and Economic Development, World Development, Tourism Management, Asia Pacific Economic Literature, Review of Economics and Finance, Energy Economics, Journal of Rural Studies, Journal of Immigrant and Refugee Studies, Journal of Economic Policy Reform, International Journal of Contemporary Hospitality Management, Australian Journal of Agricultural and Resource Economics, Agricultural Economics, Energy Economics, Journal of Small Business Management, Currently, Dr Agbola is Editor-in-Chief of African Journal of Technical Education and Management, Associate Editor of Journal of Small Business Management, Guest Editor for Tourism Economics, Guest Editor for Economies, Editorial Board Member of Tourism Economics, Journal of Hospitality and Tourism Research, African Journal of Agricultural and Resource Economics, Contemporary Management Research, and Economies. Dr Agbola consulted for Food and Agriculture Organisation, Rome and Grains Research Committee of Western Australia.

Amir Mahmood is the Dean of Western Sydney Business School. He holds a Master and a PhD in Economics from the University of Manitoba, Canada. Before joining Western Sydney University, he was the Pro Vice-Chancellor and the Chief Executive Officer of the University of Newcastle (UON) in Singapore. Prior to his UON Singapore appointment, he held a number of senior academic leadership positions at UON, including the interim Pro Vice-Chancellor (Business & Law), Deputy Head of Faculty (Business & Law), Interim Pro Vice-Chancellor

(International & Advancement), Assistant Dean International, Director Executive and Corporate Programs, Deputy and interim Head of Newcastle Graduate School of Business. Dr Mahmood is an established leader in the area of internationalisation of higher education. As a recipient of the Australian Government Endeavour Malaysia Research Fellowship, Dr. Mahmood has an active research track record in the field of economics, business and management. His research excellence is reflected in his research leadership and outcomes, which include edited books and book chapters, refereed journal articles, conference papers, invited addresses to international forums, PhD research supervision, and collaborative research projects and grants. His recent engaged research with impact include work in areas such as SMEs in Malaysia and Indonesia, mental health and productivity in Singapore, microfinance and poverty alleviation in the Philippines, disaster management in South Asia, and international trade in services in the ASEAN region.

REFERENCES

Aaby, N. & Slater, S. F. 1989, Management Influences on Export Performance: A Review of the Empirical Literature 1978-1988, *International Marketing Review*, Vol. 6, Issue 4, pp. 7-27.

Abdel-Malek, T. Export Marketing Orientation in Small Firms, *American Journal of Small Business*, Vol. 3, Issue 1, pp. 25-34.

Acs, Z. J. & Preston, L. 1997, Small And Medium-Sized Enterprises, Technology, and Globalisation: Introduction to a Special Issue on Small and Medium-Sized Enterprises in the Global Economy, *Small Business Economics*, Vol. 9, Issue 1, pp. 1-6.

ADB (Asian Development Bank) 2004, Asia Foundation, and Swiss Contact (forthcoming). *SMEs After the Crisis: The Role of Export-Oriented SMEs*. ADB: Indonesia Resident Mission, Jakarta.

ADB (Asian Development Bank) 2006, *Indonesia 2006-2009*, Country Strategy and Program, viewed 18 January 2010, <http://www.aseansec.org/pdf/sme_policies_1.pdf>

Agarwal, S. & Ramaswami, S.N. 1992, Choice of Foreign Market Entry Mode: Impact of Ownership, Location and Internationalisation Factor, *Journal of International Business Studies*, Vol. 23, Issue 1, pp. 1-27.

Aggrey, N., Eliab, L. & Joseph, S. 2010, Determinants of Export Participation in East African Manufacturing Firms, *Current Research Journal of Economic Theory*, Vol. 2, Issue 2, pp. 55-61.

Ahmed, Z. U., Julian, C. C., Baalbaki, I. & Hadidian, T. V. 2004, Export Barriers and Firm Internationalisation: A Study of Lebanese Entrepreneurs, *Journal of Management & World Business Research*, Vol. 1, Issue 1, pp. 11-22.

Albaum, G., Strandskov, J. & Duerr, E. 1998, *International Marketing and Export Development*, Addison-Wesley Longman, England.

Alexandrides, C. B. 1971, How the Major Obstacles to Expansion can be Overcome, *Atlanta Economic Review*, Vol. 21, Issue 5, pp. 12-15.

Altintas, M. H., Tokol, T., & Harcar, T. 2007, The Effects of Export Barriers on Perceived Export Performance: An Empirical Research on SMEs in Turkey, *EuroMed Journal of Business*, Vol. 2, Issue 1, pp. 36-56.

Andersen, O. 1993, On the Internationalisation Process of the Firms, A Critical Analysis, *Journal of International Business Studies*, Vol. 24, Issue 2, pp. 209-231.

Anderson, K. 2005, Setting the Trade Policy Agenda: What Roles for Economists? *World Bank Policy Research Working Paper* No. 3560.

Anderson, J. C. & Gerbing, D. W. 1988, Some Methods for Respecifying Measurement Models to Obtain Unidimensional Construct Measurement, *Journal of Marketing Research*, Vol. 19, Issue 1, pp. 453-460.

Anonymous, 1996, The Miracle of Trade, *The economist*, 27 January 1996.

ANU, Australian National University, National Asia Pacific Economic and Scientific (NAPES) Database, viewed June 2009, http://napes.anu.edu.au.virtual.anu.edu.au/

Arthur, W. B. 1990, Competing Technologies, Increasing Returns, and Lock-in by Historic Events, *Economic Journal*, Vol. 99, pp. 116-131.

Asia Foundation 2009, Asia's Economic Recovery: Constrasting Narratives, viewed June 2009, <asiafoundation.org/...asia/.../asias-economic-recovery-contrasting-narratives/>.

Aswicahyono, H. & Feridhanusetyawan, T. The Evolution and Upgrading of Indonesia's Industry, viewed June 2007, <http://www.csis.or.id/papers/wpe073>

Athukorala, P. 2006, Post-crisis Export Performance: The Indonesian Experience in Regional Perspective, *Bulletin of Indonesian Economic Studies*, Vol. 42, Issue 2, pp. 177-211.

Aulakh, P. S. & Kotabe, M. 2000, Export Strategies and Performance of Firms from Emerging Economies: Evidencefrom Latin America, *Academy of Management Journal*, Vol. 43, Issue 3, pp. 342-361.

Axinn, C. N. 1988, Export Performance: Do Managerial Perceptions Make a Difference? *International Marketing Review*, Vol. 5, Issue 2, pp. 61-71.

Axinn, C. N. 1985, *An Examination of Factors that Influence Export Performance*, Unpublished PhD Dissertation, East Lansing, Michigan State University.

Axinn, C. N. & Matthyessens, P. 2002, Limits of Internationalisation Theories in an Unlimited World, *International Marketing Review*, Vol. 19, Issue 5, pp. 436-449.

Bappenas, Badan Perencanaan dan Pembangunan Nasional, viewed January 2016, <http://els.bappenas.go.id/upload/kliping/Neraca-MI.pdf>

Bappenas, Badan Perencanaan dan Pembangunan Nasional, viewed January 2018, <http://www.bappenas.go.id/get-file-server/node/1119/>

Bagchi-Sen, S. 1999, The Small and Medium Sized Exporters' Problems: An Empirical Analysis of Canadian Manufacturers, *Regional Studies*, Vol. 33, Issue 3, pp. 231-245.

Bagozzi, R. P. 1991, Further Thoughts on the Validity of Measures of Elation, Gladness, and Joy, *Journal of Personality and Social Psychology*, Vol. 61, Issue 1, pp. 98-104.

Barabba, V. P. & Zaltman, G. 1991, Competitive Advantage through Creative Use of Marketing Information, *Hearing the Voice of the Market*, Harvard Business School Press, Boston, MA.

Barker, A. T. & Kaynak, E. 1992, An Empirical Investigation of the Differences Between Initiating And Continuing Exporters, *European Journal of Marketing*, Vol. 26, Issue 3, pp. 27-36.

Barret, N. I. & Wilkinson, I. F. 1986, Internationalisation Behavior: Management Characteristics of Australian Manufacturing Firms by Level of International Development, in Turnbull P. W. & Paliwoda S. J., editors, *Research In International Marketing*, Croom Helm, London, pp. 213-233.

Bartlett, C. A. & Ghoshal, S. 2000, *Transnational Management: Text, Cases, and Readings in Cross-border Management*, Irwin/McGraw Hill, Boston.

Basile, R. 2001, Export Behaviour of Italian Manufacturing Firms Over the Nineties: The Role of Innovation, *Research Policy*, Vol. 30, Issue 8, pp. 1185-1201.

Basri, M. C. & Van der Eng, P. 2002 Business in Indonesia: New Challenges, Old Problems, Institute of SouthEast Asian Studies, Singapore.

Beamish, P. W., Craig, R. & McLellan, K. 1993, The Performance Characteristics of Canadian versus U.K. Exporters in Small and Medium Sized Firms, *Management International Review*, Vol. 33, Issue 2, pp. 121-137.

Bell, J. 1995, The Internationalisation of Small Computer Software Firms: A Further Challenge to 'Stage' Theories, *European Journal of Marketing*, Vol. 29, Issue 8, pp. 60-75.

Bell, J., McNaughton, R., Young, S. & Crick, D. 2003, Towards an Integrative Model of Small Firms Internationalisation, *Journal of International Entrepreneurship*, Vol. 1, Issue 4, pp. 339-362.

Benito, G. & Gripsurd, G. 1992, *The Expansion of Foreign Direct Investment: Discrete Rational Location Choices or a Cultural Learning Process*, Vol. 23, Issue 3, pp. 461-476.

Bentler, P. M. & Bonnet D. G. 1980, Significance Tests and Goodness of Fit in the Analysis of Covariance Structures, *Psychological Bulletin*, Vol. 88, Issue 1, pp. 588-606.

Berry, A. & Nugent J. B. 1999, *Fulfilling the Export Potential of Small and Medium Firms*, Kluwer Academic Publishers, Boston, MA.

Berry, A., Rodriguez, E. & Sandee, H. 2001, Small and Medium Enterprise Dynamics in Indonesia, *Bulletin of Indonesian Economic Studies*, Vol. 37, Issue 5, pp. 363-384.

Berry, A., Rodriguez, E. & Sandee, H. 2002, Firm and Group Dynamics in the Small and Medium Enterprise Sector in Indonesia, *Small Business Economics*, Vol. 18, Issue 1/3, 141-161.

Berry, M. M. J. & Brock, J. K. 2004, Marketspace and Internationalisation Process of the Small Firm, *Journal of International Entrepreneurship*, Vol. 2, Issue 3, pp. 187-216.

Bilkey, W. J. 1978, An Attempted Integration of the Literature on the Export Behavior of Firms, *Journal of International Business Studies*, Vol. 7, pp. 33-46.

Bilkey, W. J. 1970, *Industrial Stimulation*, Lexington, MA: Heath Lexington Books, D. C. Heath and Company, pp. 95-100.

Bilkey, W. J. & Tesar G. 1977, The Export Behavior of Smaller-Sized Wisconsin Manufacturing Firms, *Journal of International Business Studies*, Vol. 8, pp. 93- 98.

Bodur, M. 1986, A Study on the Nature and Intensity of Problems Experienced by Turkish Exporting Firms in Cavusgil, S. T., *Advances in International Marketing 1*, editor, Greenwich, JAI Press, pp. 205-232.

Bollen, K. A. 1989, *Structural Equations with Latent Variables*, John Wiley and Sons, New York.

Bollen, K. A. & Long, J. S. 1993, *Testing Structural Equation Models,* CA: Sage, Beverly Hills.

Bonaccorsi, A. 1992, On the Relationship between Firm Size and Export Intensity, *Journal of International Business Studies*, Vol. 23, Issue 4, pp. 605-635.

Boter, H. & Holmquist, C. 1996, Industry Characteristics and Internationalisation Processes in Small Firms, *Journal of Business Venturing*, Vol. 11, Issue 6, pp. 471-487Bourke, I.J. & Leitch, J. 1998, *Trade Restrictions and Their Impact on International Trade in Forest Products*, FAO, Rome.

Bourke, I. J. & Leitch, J. 1998, *Trade Restrictions and Their Impact on International Trade in Forest Products*, FAO, Rome.

Bollen, K. A. & Long, J. S. 1993, *Testing Structural Equation Modeling*, CA: Sage, Newbury Park.

Booth, A. 1998, *The Indonesian Economy in the Nineteenth and Twentieth Centuries: A History of Missed Opportunities*, Macmillan, London.

Bradley, F. 1995, The Service Firm in International Marketing, in Glynn, W.J. & Barnes, J.G., editors, *Understand Services Management*, John Wiley & Sons, New York, NY and Chichester, pp. 420-448.

Bradshaw, R. & Burridge, M. 2001, Practices of Successful Small and Medium-sized Exporters: The Use of Market Information, *Journal of Small Business and Enterprise Development*, Vol. 8, Issue 3, pp. 267-273.

Brooks, M. & Rosson, P. 1982, A Study of Export Behavior of Small and Medium-Sized Manufacturing Firms in Three Canadian Provinces in Czinkota, M. R. & Tesar, G., editors, *Export management - An International Context*, editors, Praeger Publishers, New York, pp. 39-54.

Burton, F. N. & Schlegelmilch, B. B. 1987, Profile Analysis of Non-exporters versus Exporters Grouped by Export Involvement, *Management International Review*, Vol. 27, Issue 1, pp. 38-49.

Byrne, B. M. 2009, *Structural Equation Modeling with AMOS: Basic Concepts, Applications, and Programming*, Routledge/Taylor & Francis, New York.

Calof, J. L. 1994, The Relationship Between Firms Size and Export Behavior Revisited, *Journal of International Business Studies*, Second Quarter, pp. 367-387.

Cannon, T. 1980, Managing International and Export Marketing. *European Journal of Marketing*, Vol. 14, Issue 1, pp. 34-49.

Cannon T. & Willis, M. 1981, The Smaller Firm in International Trade, *European Small Business Journal*, Vol. 1, Issue 3, pp. 45-55.

Cateora, P. R. & Graham, J. L. 1999, *International Marketing*, 10th edition, Irwin MCGraw-Hill, Boston, MA.

Cavusgil, S. T. & Nevin, J. R. 1980, A Conceptualisation of the Initial Involvement in International Marketing, in Lamb Jr., C. W. & P. M. Dunne, editors, *Theoretical Developments in Marketing*, pp. 68-71, American Marketing Association, Chicago.

Cavusgil, S. T. 1984, Differences Among Exporting Firms Based on Their Degree of Internationalisation, *Journal of Business Research*, Vol. 12, Issue 2, pp. 195-208.

Cavusgil, S. T. 1982, On the Nature of Decision Making for Export Marketing, in Bush, R. F. & S. D. Hunt, *Marketing Theory: Philosophy of Science Perspectives*, editors, American Marketing Association, Chicago, pp. 117-180.

Cavusgil, S. T. & Nevin, J. N. 1981, Internal Determinants of Export Marketing Bevahiour: An Empirical Investigation, *Journal of Marketing Research*, Vol. 18, Issue 1, pp. 114-119.

Cavusgil, S. T. & Naor, J. 1987, Firm and Management Characteristics as Discriminators of Export Marketing Activity, *Journal of Business Research*, Vol. 15, Issue 3, pp. 221-235.

Chang, T. L. 1990, *The Competitive Strategies of Firms in Their Internationalisation Process: The Case of Taiwanese Firms in the Information Industry*, PhD Dissertation, The George Washington University, Washington DC.

Chen, M. J. 1996, Competitor Analysis and Interfirm Rivalry: Toward a Theoretical Integration, *Academy of Management Review*, Vol. 21, Issue 1, pp. 100-134.

Cheong, W. K. & Chong, K. W. 1988, Export Behavior of Small Firms in Singapore, *International Small Business Journal*, Vol. 6, Issue 2, pp. 34-41.

Chetty, S. K. & Hamilton, R. T. 1996, The Process of Exporting in Owner-Controlled Firms, *International Small Business Journal*, Vol. 14, Issue 2, pp. 12-25.

Chetty, S. K. & Hamilton, R. T. 1993, Firm-Level Determinants of Export Performance: A Meta-Analysis, *International Marketing Review*, Vol. 10, Issue 3, pp. 26-35.

Chowdhury, A. R. 1993, Does Exchange Rate Volatility Depress Trade Flows? Evidence from Error-Correction Models, *The Review of Economics and Statistics*, Vol. 75, Issue 4, pp. 700-706.

Christensen, C. H., da Rocha, A., & Gertner, R. K. 1987, An Empirical Investigation of the Factors Influencing Exporting Success of Brazilian Firms, *Journal of International Business Studies*, Vol. 18, Issue 3, pp. 61-77.

Clark, T. 1991, Review of the Competitive Advantage of Nations, by M. E. Porter, *Journal of Marketing,* Issue October, pp. 118-120.

Clarke, G. R. G. 2005, *Beyond Tariff and Quotas: Why Don't African Manufacturing Enterprises Export More*, World Bank Policy Research Working Paper 3617.

Comrey, A. L. 1978, Common Methodological Problems in Factor Analytic Studies, *Journal of Consulting and Clinical Psychology*, Vol. 46, Issue 1, pp. 648-659.

Congdon, T. 1990, Autumn books....should be made of Sterner Stuff: The Competitive Advantage of Nations, *Spectator*, Vol. 265, Issue 8463, pp. 41-42.

Corden, W. M. 1994, *Economic Policy, Exchange Rates, and the International System*. Oxford University Press, New York.

Coviello, N. E. & Munro, H. 1997, Network Relationships and the Internationalisation Process of Small Software Firms, *International Business Review*, Vol. 6, Issue 4, pp. 361-386.

Coviello, N. E. & Munro, H. 1995, Growing the Entrepreneurial Firm: Networking for International Market Development, *European Journal of Marketing*, Vol. 29, Issue 7, pp. 49-62.Crick, D. & Chaudry, S. 1997a, Small Businesses' Motives for Exporting; The Effect of Internationalisation, *Journal of Marketing Practice: Applied Marketing*, Vol. 3, Issue 3, pp. 156-171.

Crick, D. 1995, An Investigation into the Targeting of U.K. Export Assistance, *European Journal of Marketing*, Vol 29, Issue 8, pp. 76-94.

Crick, D., Al Obaidi, M. & Chaudry, S. 1998, Perceived Obstacles of Saudi-Arabian Exporters of Non-oil Products, *Journal of Marketing Practice: Applied Marketing Science*, Vol. 4, Issue 7, pp. 187-199.

Crick, D. & Chaudry, S. 2000, UK Agricultural Exporters' Perceived Barriers and Government Assistance Requirements, *Marketing Intelligence & Planning*, Vol. 18, Issue 1, pp. 30-38.

Crick, D. & Chaudry, S. 1997a, Small Businesses' Motives for Exporting; The Effect of Internationalisation, *Journal of Marketing Practice: Applied Marketing*, Vol. 3, Issue 3, pp. 156-171.

Crick, D. & Chaudry, S. 1997b, Export Problems and Government Assistance Required by UK Exporters: An Investigation into the Effect of Ethnicity, *International Journal of Entrepreneurial Behavior and Research*, Vol. 3, Issue 1, pp. 3-18.

Crick, D. & Chaudry, S. 1996, Export Behaviour of Asian and Indigenous-owned SMEs in the UK Clothing Industry: A Reseach Note, *International Journal of Entrepreneurial Behavior and Research*, Vol. 2, Issue 1, pp. 77-84.

Crick, D. & Czinkota, M. R. 1995, Export Assistance: Another Look at Whether We are Supporting the Best Programs, International Marketing Review, Vol 12, Issue 3, pp. 61-72.

Cunningham, E. 2007, *Structural Equation Modeling Using AMOS*, Education and Statistics Consultancy, Statsline, Victoria, Australia

Cushman, D. O. 1988, Exchange-rate Uncertainty and Foreign Direct Investment in the United States, *Review of World Economics*, Vol. 124, Issue 2, pp. 322-336.

Czinkota, M .R. 1982, *Export Development Strategies: U.S. Promotion Policy,* Praeger Publishers, New York.

Czinkota, M. R. & Johnston, W. J. 1983, Exporting: Does Sales Volume Make a Difference? *Journal of International Business Studies*, Vol. 14, Issue 1, pp. 147-153.

Czinkota, M. R, Ronkainen, I. A., & Moffett, M. H. 2003, *International Business*, Dryden Press, Fort Worth.

Czinkota, M. R. & Ronkainen, I. A. 1998, *International Marketing*, Dryden Press, Fort Worth.

Czinkota, M. R, Ronkainen, I. A., & Rivoli, P. 1992, *International Business*, Dryden Press, Fort Worth.

Czinkota, M. R, & Ursic, M. 1991, Classification of Exporting Firms According to Sales and Growth into a Share Matrix, *Journal of Business Research*, Vol. 22, Issue 3, pp. 243-53.

Daniels, J. D. & Guyburo, J. 1976, The Exporter – Non-exporter Interface: A Search for Variables, *Foreign Trade Review*, Vol. 1, Issue 3, pp. 258-282.

Da Rocha, A., Christensen, C. H., & Cunha, C. E. 1990, Aggressive and Passive Exporters: A study in Brazilian Furniture Industry, International Marketing Review, Vol. 7 Issue 5, pp. 6-15.

Da Silva, P. A., & Da Rocha, A. 2008, Do Perceived Export Barriers Change over Time? A Longitudinal Study of Brazilian Exporters of Manufactured Goods, *American Business Review*, Vol. 9, Issue 1, pp. 102-128.

Da Silva, P. A., & Da Rocha, A. 2001, Perceptions of Export Barriers to Mercosur by Brazilian Firms, *International Marketing Review*, Vol. 18, Issue 6, pp. 589-610.

Davis, P. S. & Harveston, P. D. 2000, Internationalisation and Organisational Growth: The Impact of Internet Usage and Technology Involvement Among Entrepeneurled Family Businesses, *Family Business Review*, Vol. 13, Issue 2, pp. 107-120.

Deephouse, D. L. 1999, To be Different or to be the Same? It's a Question (and Theory) of Strategic Balance, *Strategic Management Journal*, Vol. 20, Issue 2, pp. 147-166.

De Toni A. F. & Nassimbeni, G. 2001, The Export Propensity of Small Firms: A Comparison of Organisational and Operational Management Levers in Exporting and Non-Exporting Units, *International Journal of Entrepreneurial Behaviour & Research,* Vol. 7, Issue 4, pp. 132-147.

Diamantopoulos, A. & Inglis K. 1988, Identifying Differences between High and Low Involvement Exporters, *International Marketing Review*, Vol. 5, Issue 2, pp. 52-60.

Diamantopoulos, A. & Schlegelmilch, B. B. 1997, *Taking the Fear Out of Data*, The Dryden Press, London, UK.

Diamantopoulos, A., Schlegelmilch, B. B. & Allpress, C. 1990, Export Marketing Research in Practice: A Comparison of Users and Non-users, *Journal of Marketing Management*, Vol. 6, Issue 3, pp. 257-274.

Diamantopoulos, A. Schlegelmilch, B.B. & Tse, K.Y. 1993, Understanding the Role of Export Marketing Assistance: Empirical Evidence and

Research Needs, *European Journal of Marketing*, Vol. 27, Issue 4, pp. 5-18.

Diamantopoulos A. & Souchon, A.L. 1998, Information Utilisation by Exporting Firms: Conceptualisation, Measurement, and Impact on Export Performance, in Urban, S. et al., editors, *Information and Management: Utilisation of Technology* – Structural and Cultural Impact, Gabler, Wiesbaden, pp. 112-135.

Dichtl, E., Leibold, M., Koglmayr, H. & Muller, S. 1984, The Export Decision of Small and Medium-sized Firms: A Review, *Management International Review,* Vol. 24, Issue 2, pp. 49-60.

Dichtl, E., Koeglmayr, H. & Mueller, S. 1990, International Orientation as a Precondition for Export Success, *Journal of International Business Studies*, Vol. 21, Issue 1, pp. 23-40.

Dick, H, Houben, V. J. H., Lindblad, J. T. & Wie, T. K. 2002, *The Emergence of a National Economy: An Economic History of Indonesia, 1800-2000*, University of Hawai'I Press, Honolulu.

Dicken, P. & Lloyd, P. E. 1990, *Location in Space: Theoretical Perspectives in Economic Geography*, Harper Collins, New York.

Dollar, D. & Kraay, A. 2004, Trade, Growth, and Poverty, *The Economic Journal*, Vol 114, Issue 493, pp. F22-F49.

Dominguez, L. V. & Sequeira, C. G. 1993, Determinants of LDC Exporters Performance: A Cross-National Study, *Journal of International Business Studies*, Vol. 24, Issue1, pp. 19-40.

Donthu, N. & Kim, S. H. 1993, Implications of Firm Controllable Factors on Export Growth, *Journal of Global Marketing*, Vol. 7, Issue 1, pp. 47-63.

Down, S. 2010. *Enterprise, Entrepreneurship and Small Business*, Sage Publications Ltd, London.

Economist Intelligence Units, 2008, *the Economist Intelligence Units,* Indonesia, viewed 7 March 2008, <http://www.economist.com/countries/indonesia/profile.cfm?folder=Profile-FactSheet>

Edmund, S. E. & Khoury, S. J. 1986, Exports: A Necessary Ingredient in the Growth of Small Business Firms, *Journal of Small Business Management*, Vol. 24, Issue 4, pp. 54-65.

Edmund, S. & Sarkis, K. 1986, Export: A Necessary Ingredient in the Growth of Small Business Firms, *Journal of Small Business Management*, Vol. 24, Issue 4, pp. 54-65.

Edwards, S. 1998, Openness, Productivity and Growth: What Do We Really Know? *Economic Journal*, Vol. 108, Issue March, pp. 383-398.

Eilon, S. 1990, On Competitiveness, *Omega: International Journal of Management Science*, Vol. 20, pp. i-iv.

Ellis, P. & Pecotich, A. 2002, Macromarketing and International Trade: Comparative Advantage versus Cosmopolitan Considerations, *Journal of Macromarketing,* Vol. 22, Issue 1, pp. 35-56.

Enderwick, P. & Akoorie, M. 1994, Pilot Study Research Note: The Employment of Foreign Language Specialists and Export Success – The Case of New Zealand, *International Marketing Review*, Vol. 11, Issue 4, pp. 4-18.

Erramilli, M. K. & Rao, C. P. 1993, Service Firms' International Entry-Mode Choice: A Modified Transaction-Cost Analysis Approach, *Journal of Marketing*, Vol. 57, Issue 1, pp. 19-38.

Erwidodo 1999, *Effects of Trade Liberalisation on Agriculture in Indonesia: Institutional and Structural Aspects*, Working Paper Series 41, Bogor, United Nations Regional Coordination Centre for Course Grains, Pulses, Roots and Tuber Crops in the Humid Tropics of Asia and the Pacific (CGPRT centre).

Eshghi, A. 1992, Attitude Behavior Inconsistency in Exporting, *International Marketing Review*, Vol. 9, Issue 3, pp. 40-61.

Fillis, I. 2001, Small Firm Internationalisation: An Investigative Survey and Future Research Directions, *Management Decision*, Vol. 39, Issue 9, pp. 767-783.

Fischer, E. & Reuber, R. 2003, Targeting Export Support to SMEs: Owners' International Experience as a Segmentaion Basis, *Small Business Economics*, Vol. 20, Issue 1, pp. 69.82.

Ford, I. D. & Leonidou, L. C. 1991, Research Development in International Marketing, in Paliwoda, S.J. editor, *New Perspectives on International Marketing*, Routledge, London, pp. 3-32.

Fornell, C. & Larcker, D. 1981, Evaluating Structural Equation Models with Unobservable Variable and Measurement Error, *Journal of Marketing Research*, Vol.18, Issue, pp. 39-50.

Frazier, G. Gill, J. & Kale, S. 1989, Dealer Dependent Levels and Reciprocal Actions in a Channel of Distribution in Developing Country, *Journal of Marketing*, Vol. 53, Issue 1, pp. 50-69.

Fryges, H. 2006, *Hidden Champions – How Young and Small Technology-Oriented Firms Can Attain High Export-Sales Ratios*, ZEW Discussion Papers 06-45.

Gankema, G., Snuif, H. & Dijken, V. 1997, The Internationalisation Process of Small and Medium Sized Enterprises: An Evaluation of the Stage Theory, in Donckels, R. & Miettinen, A., editors, *Entrepreneurship and SME Research: On Its Way to the Next Millenium*, Ashgate, Aldershot.

Garnier, G. 1982, Comparative Export Behavior of Small Canadian Firms in the Printing and Electrical Industries, in Czinkota, M. R. & Tesar, G. editors, *Export Management: An International Context*, Praeger Publishers, New York, pp. 113-131.

Gencturk, E. F & Kotabe, M. 2001, The Effect of Export Assitance Program Usage on Export Performance: A Contingency Explanation, *Journal of International Marketing*, Vol. 9, Issue 2, pp. 51-72.

Gerber, J. 2005, *International Economics*, 3rd edition, Pearson Addison Wesley.

Gomez-Mejia, L. R. 1988, The Role of Human Resources Strategy in Export Perfromance: A Longitudinal Study, *Strategic Management Journal,*Vol. 9, Issue 1, pp. 493-505.

Gorsuch, R. L. 1983, *Factor Analysis* (2nd edition), NJ: Erlbaum, Hillsdale.

Gray, B. J. Profiling Managers to Improve Export Promotion Targeting, *Journal of International Business Studies*, Vol. 28, Issue 2, pp. 387-420.

Green, R. & Larsen, T. 1987, Environmental Shock and Export Opportunity, *International Marketing Review*, Vol. 4, Issue 4, pp. 30-42.

Greenaway, D. & Milner, C. 1986, *The Economics of IIT*, Basil Blackwell, Oxford.

Greenaway, D. & Tharakan, P. K. M. 1986, *Imperfect Competition and International Trade, The Policy Aspects of Intra-Industry Trade*, Wheatsheaf, Sussex.

Grimwade, N. 2000, *International Trade: New Patterns of Trade, Production & Investment*, Routledge, London.

Gripsrud, G. 1990, The Determinants of Export Decisions and Attitudes to a Distant Market: Norwegian Fishery Exports to Japan, *Journal of International Business Studies*, Vol. 21, pp. 469-485.

Gronhaug, K. & Kvitastein, O. 1992, Expansion Strategies in International Markets: An Explanatory Study, in Grunert, K.G. & Fuglene, D, editors, Marketing for Europe – Marketing for the Future, *European Marketing Academy*, Aarhus, pp. 487-504.

Grubel, H. G. & Lloyd, P. J. 1975, *Intra Industry Trade: The Theory and Measurement of Internationally Trade in Differentiated Products,* Wiley, New York

Guilford, J. P. 1954, *Psychometric Methods*, McGraw-Hill, New York.

Gupta, N. 1980, Some Alternative Definitions of Size, *Academy of Management Journal*, Vol. 23, Issue 4, pp. 759-766.

Hadad, M., Lim, J. J., & Saborowski, C. Managing Opennes and Volatility: The Role of Export Diversification, *Economic Premise*, viewed January 2010, <siteresources.worldbank.org/INTPREMNET/Resources/EP6.pdf>.

Hall, C. 2002, Profile of SMEs and SME Issues in APEC 1999-2000, final draft report, viewed 16 December 2009, <http://www.aseansec.org/pdf/sme_policies_1.pdf>

Hair, J. F. Jr., Anderson, R.E., Tatham, R.L. & Black, W.C. 1998, *Multivariate Data Analysis*, Prentice-Hall, Upper Saddle River, New Jersey.

Harveston, P. D., Kedia, B. L. & Davis, P. S. 2000, Internationalisation of Born Global and Gradual Globalizing Firms: The Impact of the Manager, *Advances in Competitiveness Research*, Vol. 8, Issue 1, pp. 92-100.

Hassler, M. 2003, Crisis, Coincidences and Strategic Market Behavior: The Internationalisation of Indonesian Clothing Brand-Owners, *Area*, Vol. 35, Issue 3, pp. 241-250.

Hayashi, M. 2002, The Role of Subcontracting in SME Development in Indonesia: Micro Level Evidence from the Metalworking and Machinery Industry, *Journal of Asian Economics*, Vol. 13, Issue 1, pp. 1-26.

Hayduk, L. A. 1996, *LISREL Issues, Debates and Strategies*, John Hopkins Press, London.

Hayduk, L. A. & Glasser, D. N. 2000, Jiving' the Four-step, Waltzing around Factor Analysis, and Other Serious Fun, *Structural Equation Modeling*, Vol. 7, Issue 1, pp. 1-35.

Hill, H. 1992, Regional Development in a Boom and Bust Petroleum Economy: Indonesia since 1970, *Economic Development and Cultural Change*, Vol. 40, Issue 2, pp. 351-379.

Hill, H. 1995a, The Economic of Recent Changes in the Weaving Industry, *Bulletin of Indonesian Economic Studies*, Vol. 16, Issue 2, pp. 83-103.

Hill, H. 1995b, Indonesia's Great Leap Forward? Technology Development and Policy Issues, *Bulletin of Indonesian Economic Studies*, Vol 31, Issue 2, pp. 83-123.

Hill, H. 1996a, Indonesia's Industrial Policy and Performance: "Orthodoxy" Vindicated, *Economic Development and Cultural Change*, Vol. 45, Issue 1, pp. 147-174.

Hill, H. 1996b, Indonesia: From 'Chronic Dropout' to 'Miracle', *Journal of International Development,* Vol. 7, Issue 5, pp. 775-789.

Hill, H. 2001, Small and Medium Enterprises in Indonesia: Old Policy Challenges for a New Administration, *Asian Survey*, Vol. 41, Issue 2, pp. 248-270.

Hill, C. W. L. 2003, *International Business: Competing in the Global Marketplace*, 4th edition, McGraw-Hil/Irwin, New York, USA.

Hirsch, S. & Lev, B. 1971, Sales Stabilisation Through Export Diversification, *Review of Economics & Statistics*, Vol. 53, Issue 3, pp. 270-277.

Holden, A. 1986, Small Business can Market in Europe: Results from a Survey of U.S. Exporters, *Journal of Small Business Management*, Issue January, pp. 22-29.

Hooper, P. & Kohlhagen, S. W. 1978, The Effect of Exchange Rate Uncertainty on the Prices and Volume of International Trade, *Journal of International Economics*, Vol. 8, Issue 4, pp. 483-511.

Holzmuller, H. H., & Kasper, H. 1990, The Decision-maker and Export Activity: A Cross National Comparison of the Foreign Orientation of Austrian Managers, *Management International Review*, Vol. 3, Issue 3, pp. 217-230.

Holzmuller, H. H. & Kasper, H. 1991, On Theory of Export Performance: Personal and Organisational Determinants of Export Trade Activities Observed in Small and Medium-Sized Firms, *Management International Review*, Vol. 31, Issue March, pp. 45-70.

Hu, L. T. & Bentler, P. M. 1999, Cutoff Criteria for Fit Indexes in Covariance Structure Analysis: Conventional Criteria Versus New Alternatives, *Structural Equation Modeling*, Vol. 6, Issue 1, pp. 1-55.

Hu, L. T. & Bentler, P. M 1998, Fit Indices in Covariance Structure Modeling: Sensitivity to underparamerterized Model Misspecification, *Psychological Methods*, Vol. 3. Issue 1, pp. 424-453.

Humphrey, J. & Schmitz, H. 1996, The Triple C Approachto Local Industrial Policy, *World Development*, Vol. 23, Issue 1, pp. 149-162.

Hutchinson, K., Quinn, B., Alexander N. 2006, SME Retailer Internationalisation: Case Study Evidence from British Retailers, *International Marketing Review*, Vol. 23, Issue 1, pp. 25-53.

Ibeh, K. I. N. & Young, S. 2001, Exporting as an Entrepreneurial Act: An Empirical Study of Nigerian Firms, *European Journal of Marketing*, Vol. 35, Issue5/6, pp. 566-586.

Ibeh, K. I. N., Ibrahim, E. & Ezepue, P. O. 2007, Factors Stimulating Initial Export Activity, *Journal of African Business*, Vol. 8, Issue 2, pp 7-26.

Indonesian Ministry of Cooperative and SMEs 2010, viewed 18 January 2010, <http://www.depkop.go.id/cat_view/35-statistik/37-statistik-ukm/186-statistik-ukm-2007.html>

Isgut, A. 2001, What's Different about Exporters? Evidence from Colombian Manufacturing, *Journal of Development Studies*, Vol. 37, Issue 5, pp. 57-82.

Jaffe, E., Nebenzabl, H. & Pasternak, I. D. 1988, The Export Behavior of Small and Mediumsized Israeli Manufacturers, *Journal of Global Marketing*, Vol. 2, Issue 2, pp. 27-49.

Jain, S. C. 1989, Standardisation of International Marketing Strategy: Some Research Hypotheses, *Journal of Marketing*, Vol. 53, Issue 1, 70-79.

Jannson, H. & Sandberg, S 2008, Internationalisation of Small and Medium-Sized Enterprises in the Baltic Sea Region, *Journal of International Management*, Vol. 14, Issue 1 , pp. 65-77.

Janzen, S. S. & Frost, J. 2000, Alberta Non-Tariff Trade Barriers Study, *Western Centre for Economic Research paper*, Issue 58, November.

Jeannet, J. P. & Hennessey, D. H. 1998, *Global Marketing Strategies*, Houghton Mifflin Company, Boston.

Johanson, J. & Mattson, L. 1988, Internationalisation in Industrial Systems – A Network Approach, in Hood, N. & Vahlne, J.E., editors, *Strategies in Global Competition*, Croom Helm, Kent.

Johanson, J. & Vahlne, J. E. 1977, The Internationalisation Process of the Firm – A Model of Knowledge Development and Increasing Foreign Market Commitments, *Journal of International Business Studies*, Vol. 8, Issue 1, pp. 23-32.

Johanson, J. & Wiedersheim-Paul, F. 1975, The Internationalisation of the Firm – Four Swedish Cases, *Journal of International Management Studies*, Vol. 12, Issue 3, pp. 305-322.

Johnston, W. J. & Czinkota, M. R. 1982, Managerial Motivations as Determinants of Industrial Export Behavior, in Czinkota M. R. & G. Tesar, Editors, Export *Management: An International Context*, Praeger Publishers, New York

Joreskog K. G. & Sorbom, D. 1984, *LISREL VI (Computer Software),* IL: Scientific Software International Inc, Chicago.

Joreskog K. G. & Sorbom, D. 1993, *LISREL VI (Computer Software),* IL: Scientific Software International Inc, Chicago.

Joynt, P. 1982, An Empirical Study of Norwegian Export Behavior, in Czinkota M. R. , & Tesar G. editors, *Export management - An International Context*, editors, Praeger Publishers, New York, pp. 55-69.

Julian, C. & O'Cass, A. 2004, The Impact of Firm and Environment Characteristics on International Joint Venture (IJV) Marketing Performance in Thailand, *International Business Review*, Vol. 46, Issue 4, pp. 359-380.

Kaleka, A. & Katsikeas, C. S. 1995, Exporting Problems: The Relevance of Export Development, Journal of Marketing Management, Vol. 11, Issue 5, pp. 499-515.

Kalwani, M. U. & Narayandas, N. 1995, Long-term Manufacturer-Supplier Relationship: Do They Pay Off for Supplier Firms? *Journal of Marketing*, Vol. 59, Issue1, pp. 1-16.

Katsikeas, C. S. 2003, Advance in International Marketing: Theory and Practice, *International Business Review*, Vol. 12, Issue 1, pp. 135-140.

Katsikeas, C. S. 1994, Perceived Export Problems and Export Involvement: The Case of Greek Exporting Manufacturers, *Journal of Global Marketing*, Vol. 7, Issue 4, pp. 29-57.

Katsikeas C. S. 1994b, Export Competitive Advantages: The Relevance of Firm Characteristics, *International Marketing Review*, Vol 11, Issue 3, pp. 33-53.

Katsikeas, C. S. & Piercy, N. F. 1991, The Relationship between Exporters from a Developing Country and Importers based in Developed Country: Conflict Considerations, *European Journal of Marketing*, Vol. 25, Issue 1, pp. 6-25.

Katsikeas, C S. & Piercy, N. F. 1993, Long-term Export Stimuli and Firm Characteristics in a European LDC, *Journal of International Marketing*, Vol. 1, Issue 3, pp. 23-47.

Katsikeas, C. S. & Morgan, R. E. 1994, Differences in Perceptions of Exporting Problems based on Firm Size and Export Market Experience, *European Journal of Marketing*, Vol. 28, Issue 5, pp. 17-35.

Katsikeas, C. S. 1996, Ongoing Export Motivation: Differences between Regular and Sporadic Exporters, *International Marketing Review*, Vol. 13, Issue 2, pp. 4-19.

Katsikeas, C. S., Leonidou, L. C, & Morgan, N. A. 2000, Firm-level Performance Assessment: Review, Evaluation, and Development, *Journal of the Academy of Marketing Science*, Vol. 28, Issue 4, pp. 493-511.

Kaynak, E. 1982, Marketing in the Third World, Praeger Publishing, New York, NY.

Kaynak, E. & Kothari, V. 1984, Export Behavior of Small and Medium-Sized Manufacturers: Some Policy Guidelines for International Marketers, *Management International Review*, Vol. 24, Issue 2, pp. 61-69.

Kaynak, E., Ghauri, P. N., Olofsson-Bredenlow, T. 1987, Export Behavior of Swedish Firms, *Journal of Small Business Management*, Vol. 25, Issue 2, pp. 26-32.

Kedia, B. L. & Chhokar, J. 1986, Factors inhibiting export performance of firms: an empirical investigation, *Management International Review*, Vol. 26, Issue 4, pp. 33-43.

Kenen, P. B. & Rodrik, D. 1986, Measuring and Analyzing the Effects of Short-term Volatility in Real Exchange Rates, *The Review of Economics and Statistics*, Vol. 68, Issue 2, pp. 311-315.

Keng, K. A. & Jiuan, T. S. 1989, Differences Between Small and Medium Sized Exporting and Non-Exporting Firms: Nature or Nurture, *International Marketing Review*, Vol. 6, Issue 4, pp. 27-41.

Kessides, C. 1993, *The Contributions of Infrastructure to Economic Development: A Review of Experience and Policy Implications*, World Bank, Washington D.C.

Kindra, G. S. 1984, *Marketing in Developing Countries*, Croom Helm, London.

Kingsbury, D. 2005, *The Politics of Indonesia*, Oxford University Press, South Melbourne.

Kinsey, J. 1987, Marketing and the Small Manufacturing Firm in Scotland, *Journal of Small Business Management*, Vol. 25, Issue 2, pp. 18-25.

Kim, W. C. 1987, Competition and the Management of Host Government Intervention", Sloan Management Review, Vol. 28, Issue 3, pp. 33-39.

Kirpalani V. H. & MacIntosh, N. 1980, Internal Marketing Effectiveness of Technology Oriented Small Firms, *Journal of International Business Studies*, Vol. 11, Issue Winter, pp. 81-90.

Kirpalani, V. H. & Balcome, D. 1987, International Marketing Success: On Conducting More Relevant Research, in Rosson, P.J. & Reid, S.D. editors, *Managing Export Entry and Expansion*, Praeger Publishers, New York, NY, pp. 386-397.

Klein S. & Roth V. J. 1990, Determinants of Export Channel Structure: The Effects of Experience and Psychic Distance, *International Marketing Review*, Vol. 7, Issue 5, pp. 27-38.

Knight, R. V. & Gappert, G. 1989, Cities in Global Society, *Urban Affairs Annual Review*, Vol. 35, Sage Publications, Beverly Hills, California.

Kogut, B. & Singh, H. 1988, The Effect of National Culture on the Choice of Entry Mode, *Journal of International Business Studies*, Vol. 19, Issue 3, pp. 411-432.

Kotabe, M. & Czinkota, M. R. 1992, State Government Promotion of Manufacturing Exports: A Gap Analysis, *Journal of International Business Studies*, Vol. 23, Issue 4, pp. 637-658.

Krugman, P. R. & Obstfeld, M. 2003, *International Economics: Theory and Policy*, 6th edition, Addison-Wesley, Boston, USA.

Kundu, S. & Katz, J. A. 2003, Born-international SMEs: Bi-level Impacts of Resources and Intentions, *Small Business Economics*, Vol. 20, Issue 1, pp. 25-47.

Lages, L. F. & Montgomery, D. B. 2004, Export Performance as an Antecedent of Export Commitment and Marketing Strategy Adaptation: Evidence from Small and Medium-sized Exporters, *European Journal of Marketing*, Vol. 38, Issue 9/10, pp. 1186-1214.

Lall, S. 1999. *The Technological Response to Import Liberalisation in Sub-Saharan Africa*, Macmillan Press, London.

Lambkin, M & Day, G. S. 1989, Evolutionary Processes in Competitive Markets: Beyond the Product Life Cycle, *Journal of Marketing*, Vol. 53, Issue 3, pp. 4-20.

Lecraw, D. J. 1993, Outward Direct Investment by Indonesian Firms: Motivation and Effects, *Journal of International Business Studies*, 3rd quarter, pp. 589-600.

Lee, W. Y., Brasch, J. J. 1978, The Adoption of Export as an Innovation, *Journal of International Business Studies*, Vol. 9, Issue 1, pp. 85-93.

Leonidou, L.C. 2004, An Analysis of the Barriers Hindering Small Business Export Development, Journal of Small Business Management, Vol. 24, Issue 3, pp. 279-302.

Leonidou, L. C. 1995a, Empirical Research on Export Barriers: Review, Assessment, and Synthesis, Journal of International Marketing, Vol. 3, Issue 1, pp. 29-43.

Leonidou, L. C. 1995b, Export Barriers: Non-Exporters' Perceptions. *International Marketing Review*, Vol. 12, Issue 1, pp. 4-25.

Leonidou, L. C. & Katsikeas, C. S. 1996. The Export Development Process: An Integrative Review of Empirical Models, *Journal of International Business Studies*, Vol. 27, Issue 3, pp. 517-551.

Leonidou, L.C, Katsikeas, C. S. & Samiee, S. 2002, Marketing Strategy Determinants of Export Performance: A Meta Analysis, *Journal of Business Research*, Vol. 55, Issue 1, pp. 51-67.

Leonidou, L. C., Katsikeas, C. S. & Piercy, N. 1998, Identifying Managerial Influences on Exporting: Past Research and Future Directions, *Journal of International Marketing*, Vol. 6, Issue 2, pp. 74-103.

Leontief, Wassily W. 1953. Domestic Production and Foreign Trade: The American Capital Position Re-Examined. Proceedings of the American Philosophical Society, Vol. 97, September, pp. 332-349.

Lesch, W.C., Eshghi, A. & Eshghi, G.S. 1990, A Review of Export Promotion Programs in the Ten Largest Industrial States, in Cavusgil, S.T. & Czinkota, M.R., editors, International Perspectives on Trade Promotion and Assistance, Quorum, New York, NY, pp. 25-38.

Liargovas, P. G. & Skandalis, K. S. 2008, Export Motivations and Barriers: A Case Study of Greek Firms Exporting to four South-Eastern European Countries, *Global Business and Economics Review*, Vol. 10, Issue 4, pp. 430-448.

Liedholm, C. & Mead D. 1987, Small Scale Industries in Developing Countries: Empirical Evidence and Policy Implications, *International Development Paper* No. 9, Department of Agricultural Economics, Michigan State University, East Lansing, MI. USA.

Lim, J. S., T. W. Sharkey & K. I. Kim 1991, An Empirical Test of an Export Adoption Model, Management International Review, Vol. 31, Issue 1, pp. 51-62.

Lindeman, R. H., Merenda, P. F. & Gold, R. 1980, *Introduction to Bivariate and Multivariate Analysis*, Scott, Foresman, & Co., New York.

Little, I. M., Mazumdar, D., & Page, J. M. 1987, *Small Manufacturing Enterprises: A Comparative Analysis of India and Other Economies*, Oxford University Press, New York.

Long, J. S. 1983, *Confirmatory Factor Analysis*, Sage, Beverly Hills.

Luostarinen, R. & Welch, L. 1990, *International Business Operation*, Kyriiri Oy, Helsinki.

MacCallum, R. C., Browne M. W. & Sugawara, H. M. 1996, Power Analysis and Determination of Sample Size for Covariance Structure Modeling, *Psychological Methods*, Vol. 1, Issue 1, pp. 130-149.

Madsen, T. K. 1989, Sucessful Export Marketing Management: Some Empirical Evidence, *International Marketing Review*, Vol. 6, Issue 4, pp. 41-57.

Malekzadeh, A. R. & Nahavandi, A. 1985, Small Business Exporting: Misconceptions are Abundant, *American Journal of Small Business*, Vol. 9, Issue 4, pp. 7-14.

Manning, C. 2000, Labour Market Adjustment to Indonesia's Economic Crisis: Context, Trends and Implications, *Bulletin of Indonesian Economic Studies* , Vol. 36, Issue 1, pp. 105-136.

Manolova, T. S., Brush, C. G., Edelman, L. F. & Greene, P. G. 2002, Internationalisation of Small Firms, *Internatioonal Small Business Journal*, Vol. 20, Issue 1, pp. 9-31.

Marshall, A, 1920, *Principles of Economics*, Macmillan, London.

Mathieu, J. E. Tannenbaum, S. I & Salas, E. 1992, Influences of Individual and Situational Characteristics on Measures of Training Effectiveness, *Academy of Management Journal*, Vol. 35, Issue 1, pp. 828-847.

McAuley, A. 1993, The Perceived Usefulness of Export Information Sources, *European Journal of Marketing*, Vol. 27, Issue 10, pp. 52-64.

McCawley, P. 1981, The Indonesian Economy Since the Mid Sixties, in Booth, A. & McCawley, P., editors, *The Indonesian Economy During the Suharto Era*, Oxford University Press, Kuala Lumpur.

McGuiness, N. W. & Little, B. 1981, The Influence of Product Characteristics on the Export Performance of New Industrial Product, *Journal of Marketing*, Vol. 45, Issue Spring, pp. 102-122.

Miesenbock, K. J 1988, Small Business and Exporting: A Literature Review, *International Small Business Journal*, Vol. 6, Issue 2, pp. 42-61.

Ministry of Cooperatives and SMEs (MOCSMES), viewed December 2009, http://www.depkop.go.id/depkopgoid2008/index.php/statistik-ukm/cat_view/35-statistik/37-statistik-ukm/186-statistik-ukm-2008.html.

Mintz, I. 1967, Cyclical Fluctuations in the Exports in the United States since 1879 in *A Longitudinal analysis of Total U.S. Exports*, National Bureau of Economic Research, New York.

Mittelstaedt, J. D., Ward, W. A. & Nowlin, E. 2006, Location, Industrial Concentration and the Propensity of Small Firms to Export, *International Marketing Review*, Vol. 23, Issue 5, pp. 486-503.

Moini, A. H. 1997, Barriers Inhibiting Export Performance of Small and Medium-Sized Manufacturing Firms, *Journal of Global Marketing*, Vol. 10, Issue 4, pp. 67-93.

Moon, J. & Lee, H. 1990, On the Internal Correlates of Export Stage Development : An Empirical Invetigation in the Korean Electronics Industry, *International Marketing Review*, Vol. 7, Issue 5, pp. 16-26.

Morgan, R. E. 1997. Export Stimuli and Export Barriers: Evidence from Empirical Research Studies, *European Business Review*, Vol. 97, Issue 2, pp. 68-79.

Morgan, R. E. & Katsikeas, C. S. 1997, Theories of International Trade, Foreign Direct Investment and Firm Internationalisation: A Critique. *Management Decision*, Vol. 35, Issue 1, pp. 68-78.

Mpinganjira, M. 2004, *The Determinants of Export Involvement in Small and Medium Sized Firms: The Case of Malawi*, PhD Dissertation, Newcastle Business School, University of Newcastle, Australia.

Naidu, G. M. & Rao T. R 1993, Public Sector Promotion of Exports: A Need-based Approach, *Journal of Business Research*, Vol. 27,

DGNED 2017, *Indonesian National Agency for Export Development*, Jakarta, viewed 9 March 2007, <http://djpen.kemendag.go.id/exporter.php?ctrl=propinsi>.

Ogbuehi, A. O. & Longfellow, T. A. 1994, Perceptions of U.S. Manufacturing SMEs Concerning Exporting: A Comparison Based on Export Experience, *Journal of Small Business Management*, Vol. 32, Issue4, pp. 37-47.

O'Grady, S. & Lane, H. 1996, The Psychic Distance Paradox, *Journal of International Business Studies*, Vol. 27, Issue 2, pp. 309-333.

Ogram, E. W. Jr. 1982, Exporters and Non-exporters: A Profile of Small Manufacturing Firms in Georgia, in Czinkota, M. R & Tesar G, Eds, *Export Management: An International Context*, Praeger Publishers, New York, pp. 70-84.

Ohlin, B. 1933, *Interregional and International Trade*, Harvard University Press, Cambridge.

Olson, H. C. & Wiedersheim-Paul, F. 1978, Factor Affecting the Pre-export Behavior of Non-exporting Firms, in Leontiades, J., editor, *European Research in International Business*, North Holland, Amsterdam.

Papanek, G. F. 1980, *The Indonesian Economy*, Praeger, New York.

Patterson, P. G. de Ruyter, K. & Wetzels, M. 1999, Modelling Firms' Propensity to Continue Service Exporting: A Cross-Country Analysis, *International Business Review*, Vol. 8, Issue 3, pp. 351-365.

Pavord, W. C & Bogart, R. G. 1975, The Dynamics of the Decision to Export, *Akron Business and Economic Review*, Issue: Spring, pp. 6-11.

Pedersen, T. & Petersen, B. 1998, Explaining Gradually Increasing Resource Commitment to a Foreign Market, *International Business Review*, Vol. 7, Issue 3, pp. 483-501.

Philp, N. & Wickramasekara, R. 1995, The Propensity to Export Among Food Processing Firms in Southern New South Wales and North Eastern Victoria: An Exploratory Study, *Agribusiness Review*, Vol. 3, Paper 8.

Piercy, N. F. & Cravens, D. W. 1995, The Network Paradigm and the Marketing Organisation: Developing a New Management Agenda, *European Journal of Marketing*, Vol. 29, Issue 3, pp. 7-34.

Porter, M. 1990. *The Competitive Advantage of Nations*, Graduate School of Business Administration, Harvard University, Boston, USA.

Powell, W. W. 1987, Hybrid Organisational Arrangements, *California Management Review*, Vol. 30, Issue 1, pp. 67-87.

Propenko, J. 1995, Future Management Strategies, in Propenko, J., editor, *Management for Privatisation*, International Labour Organisation, Geneva.

Pugel, T. A. & Lindert, P. H. 2000, *International Economics*, Irwin/McGraw-Hill, New York.

Rabino, S. 1980, An Examination of Barriers to Exporting Encountered by Small Manufacturing Companies, *Management International Review*, Vol. 1, pp. 67-73.

Ramaswami, S. N. & Yang, Y. 1990, Perceived Barriers to Exporting and Export Assistance Requirements, in Cavusgil, S. T. & M. R. Czinkota, *International Perspectives on Trade Promotion and Assistance*, Greenwood, UK, pp. 187-207.

Rasheed, H. S. 2005, Foreign Entry Mode Strategy and Performance; Moderating Effects of Environmental Factors, *Journal of Small Business Management*, Vol. 43, Issue 1, pp. 41-54.

Raykov, T. 1997, Estimation of Composite Reliability for Congeneric Measures, *Applied Psychological Measurement*, Vol. 18, Issue 1, pp. 63-77.

Raykov, T. 1998, Cronbach's Alpha and Reliability for Congeneric Measures, *Applied Psychological Measurement*, Vol. 21, Issue 1, pp. 173-184.

Reich, R. 1990, But Now We're Global, *Times Literary Supplement*, Issue August, pp. 925-926.

Reid, S. D. 1981, The Decision-maker and Export Entry and Expansion, *Journal of International Business Studies*, Vol. 12, Issue 2, pp. 101-112.

Reid, S. D. 1982, The Impact of Size on Export Behavior in Small Firms, in Czinkota M. R. & Tesar G., editors, *Export Management: An International Context,* Praeger Publishers, New York, pp. 18-38.

Reid, S. D. 1983, Managerial and Firm Influences on Export Behavior, *Journal of the Academy Marketing Science*, Vol. 11, Issue 3, pp. 323-332.

Reid, S. D. 1984, Information Acquisition and Export Entry Decisions in Small Firms, *Journal of Business Research*, Vol. 12, Issue 2, pp. 141-157.

Reuber, A. R. & Fischer, E. 1997, The Influence of the Management Team's International Experience on the Internationalisation Behavior of SMEs, *Journal of International Business Studies*, Vol. 28, Issue 4, pp. 807-825.

Reynolds, P. D. 1997. New and Small Firms in Expanding Markets. *Small Business Economics,* Vol. 9, Issue 1, pp. 79-84.

Rigdon, E. E. 1996, CFI Versus RMSEA: A Comparison of Two Fit Indices for Structural Equation Modeling, *Structural Equation Modeling*, Vol. 3, Issue 4, pp. 369-379.

Roberts, M. J. & Tybout, J. R. 1997, The Decision to export in Colombia: An Empirical Model of Entry with Sunk Costs, *American Economic Review*, Vol. 87, Issue 4, pp. 545-564.

Ronen, S. & Shenkar, O. 1985, Clustering Countries on Attitudinal Dimensions: A Review and Synthesis, *Academy of Management Review*, Vol. 10, Issue 3, pp. 435-454.

Ross, C. A. 1989, Exporters and Non-exporters of Manufactured Products: The Case of Jamaica, *Journal Of Global Marketing*, Vol. 3, Issue 2, pp. 77.103.

Sachs, J. & Warner, A. 1995, *Economic Reform and the Process of Global Integration*, Brookings Papers on Economic Activity.

Sagebien, J. 1990, The Competitive Advantage of Nations by M. E. Porter, *Journal of Macromarketing*, Issue Fall, pp. 94-99.

Sandee H. & Ibrahim B. 2002, *Evaluation of SME Trade and Export Promotion in Indonesia*, ADB Technical Assistance: SME Development, April.

Samiee, S. & Walters, P. G. P. 1990, Influence of Firm Size on Export Planning and Performance, *Journal of Business Research*, Vol. 20, Issue 3, pp. 235-248.

Samiee, S. & Walters, P. G. P. 1991, Segmenting Corporate Exporting Activities: Sporadic Versus Regular Exporters, *Journal of the Academy Marketing Science*, Vol. 19, Issue 2, pp. 93-104.

Samiee, S. & Walters, P. G. P. 1999, Determinants of Structured Export Knowledge Acquisition, *International Business Review*, Vol. 8, Issue 4, pp. 373-397.

Schaper, M. & Volery, T. 2004, *Entrepreneurship and Small Business: A Pacific Rim Perspective*, John Wiley & Sons Australia Ltd.

Schlegelemilch, B. B. & Ross, A. G. 1987, The Influence of Managerial Characteristics on Different Measures of Export Success, *Journal of Marketing Management*, Vol. 3, Issue 2, pp. 145-158.

Schumacker, R. E. & Lomax, R. G. 1996, *The Beginner's Guide to Structural Equation Modeling*, Lawrence Erlbaum Associates, New Jersey.

Seringhaus, F. H. R. 1986, The Impact of Government Export Marketing Assistance, *International Marketing Review*, Vol. 3 Issue 2, pp. 55-66.

Seringhaus, F. H. R. 1987, Export Promotion: The Role and Impact of Government Services, *Irish Marketing Review*, Vol. 2, Issue 1, pp. 106-116.

Seringhaus, F. H. R. & Botschen, G. 1991, Cross-national Comparison of Export Promotion Services: The Views of Canadian and Austrian Companies, *Journal of International Business Studies*, Vol. 22, Issue 1, pp. 115-133.

Seringhaus F. H. R. & Rosson, P. J. 1990, *Government Export Promotion: A Global Perspective*, Routledge, London, UK.

Sethuraman, R., Anderson, J. C. & Narus, J. A. 1988, Partnership Advantage and Its Determinants in Distributor and Manufacturers Working Relationships, *Journal of Business Research*, Vol. 17, Issue 4, pp. 327-347.

Shamsuddoha, A. K. & Ali, M. Y. 2009, Export Assistance in the Garment Industry: An Examination of Awareness, Use and Perceived Benefit, *Journal for Global Business Advancement*, Vol. 2, Issue 4, pp. 381-389.

Shoham, A. & Albaum G. S. 1995, Reducing the Impact of Barriers to Exporting: A Managerial Perspective, *Journal of International Marketing*, Vol. 3, Issue 4, pp. 85.105.

Silverman, M., Castaldi, R. M. & Sengupta, S. 2002, Increasing the Effectiveness of Export Assistance Programs, The Case of the California Environmental Technology Industry, *Journal of Global Marketing*, Vol. 15, Issue 3/4, pp. 173-192.

Simpson, C.L. & Kujawa, D. Jr. 1974, The Export Decision Process: An Empirical Inquiry, *Journal of International Business Studies*, Issue: Spring, pp. 107-117.

Sjoholm, F., Which Indonesian Firms Export? The Importance of Foreign Networks, *Papers in Regional Science*, Vol. 82, pp. 333.350.

Smith, A. 1776, *An Inquiry into the Nature And Causes of the Wealth of Nations*, United Kingdom, W. Strathan and T. Cadell, Londres.

Soesastro, H. & Atje, R. 2005, Survey of Recent Developments, *Bulletin of Indonesian Economic Studies*, Vol. 41, Issue 1, pp. 5-34.

Soesastro, H. & Basri, M. C. 2005, *The Political Economy of Trade Policy in Indonesia*, Economics Working Paper Series, viewed June 2008, http://www.csis.or.id/papers/wpe092.

Souchon, A. L. & Damantopoulos, A. 1996, A Conceptual Framework of Export Marketing Information Use: Key Issues and Research Propositions, *Journal of International Marketing*, Vol. 4, Issue 3, pp. 49-71.

Stanley, J., Ingram, D. & Chittick, C. 1989, *The Relationship between International Trade and Linguistic Competence: Report to the Australian Advisory Council on Languages and Multicultural Education*, Australian Government Publishing Service, Canberra.

Stottinger, B. & Schlegelmilch, B. B. Explaining Export Development through Psychic Distance: Enlightening or Elusive? *International Marketing Review*, Vol. 15, Issue 5, pp. 357-372.

Strange, R. & Katrak, H. 2002, *Small-scale Enterprises in Developing and Transitional Economies*, Palgrave, Basingstoke.

Suarez-Ortega, S. M. 2003, Export Barriers: Insights from Small And Medium-Sized Firms, *International Small Business Journal*, Vol. 21, Issue 4, pp. 403-420

Suarez-Ortega, S. M. & Alamo-Vera, F. R. 2005, SMEs Internationalisation: Firms and Managerial Factors, *International journal of Entrepreneurial Behavior and Research*, Vol. 11, Issue 4, pp. 258-279.

Sullivan, D. & Bauerschmidt, A. 1988, Common Factors Underlying Incentive to Export: Studies in the European Forest Products Industry, *European Journal of Marketing*, Vol. 22, Issue 10, pp. 41-55.

Sullivan, D. & Bauerschmidt, A. 1990, Common Factors Underlying Incentive to Export: Studies in the European Forest Products Industry, *European Journal of Marketing*, Vol. 22, Issue 10, pp. 41-55.

Tambunan, T. T. H. 2000, *Development of Small-Scale Industries During the New Order Government in Indonesia*, Aldershot, Ashgate.

Terpstra V. & Sarathy R. 2000, *International Marketing*, Dryden Press, Forth Worth, London.

Tharakan, P. K. M. 1983, *Intra-industry Trade: Empirical and Methodological Aspects*, Elsevier Science, Amsterdam.

Tesar, G. & Tarleton, J. 1982. Comparison of Wisconsin and Virginia small and medium-sized exporters: aggressive and passive exporters in M. Czinkota & G. *Tesar. Export Management-An International Context*, Editors, pp. 39-54, New York, Praeger.

Tesform G. & Lutz, C. 2006, A Classification of Export Marketing Problems of Small and Medium Sized Manufacturing Firms in Developing Countries, *International Journal of Emerging Markets*, Vol. 1, Issue 3, pp. 262-281.

Thomas, M. J. & Araujo, L. 1985, Theories of Export Behavior: A Critical Analysis, *European Journal of Marketing*, Vol. 19, Issue 2, pp. 42-52.

Trimeche, M. 2004, The Changing Business Environment in Tunisia: Implications for Multinationals, Journal of African Business, Vol. 5, Issue 2, pp. 71-92.

Tsai, W. M., MacMillan, I. C. & Low, M. B. 1991, Effects of Strategy and Environment on Corporate Venture Success in Industrial Markets, *Journal of Business Venturing*, Vol. 6, Issue 1, pp. 9-28.

Tseng, J. & Yu, C. M. J. 1991, Export of Industrial Goods to Europe: The Case of Large Taiwanese Firms, *European Journal of Marketing*, Vol. 25, Issue 9, pp. 51-63.

Tybout, J. R. 2000, Manufacturing Firms in Developing Countries: How Well Do They Do and Why? *Journal of Economic Literature*, Vol. 38, Issue March, pp. 11-44.

Urata, S. 2000, *Policy Recommendations for SME Promotion in the Republic of Indonesia, Report of JICA Senior Advisor to the Coordinating Minister of the Economy*, Finance and Industry, JICA, Tokyo, 26 July, pp. 16-32.

Ursic, M. L. & Czinkota, M. R. 1989, The Relationship Between Managerial Characteristics and Exporting Behavior, *Developments in Marketing Science*, Vol. 12, pp. 208-210.

Van Diermen, P. 1998, Sistem Kewirausahaan: Industri Garmen dan Furniture Kayu di Indonesia, PT Pustaka CIDESINDO Jakarta and Massey University, New Zealand.

Velicer, W. F., Peacock A. C., & Jakcson, D. N. 1982, A Comparison of Component and Factor Patterns: A Monte Carlo Approach, Multivariate *Behavioural Research*, Vol. 17, Issue 1, pp. 371-388.

Vernon, R.. 1966, International Investment and International Trade in the Product Life Cycle, *Quarterly Journal of Economics*, Vol.80, Issue 2, pp. 190-207.

Vona, S. 1991, On the Measurement of Intra-industry Trade: Some Further Thoughts, *Review of World Economics*, Vol. 127, Issue 4, pp. 678-700.

Wade, R. H. 2003, What Strategies are Viable for Developing Countries today? The World Trade Organisation and the Shrinking of 'Development Space' *Review of International Political Economy*, Vol. 10, Issue 4, pp. 621-644.

Wakelin, K. 1998, Innovation and Export Behaviour at the Firm Level, *Research Policy*, Vol. 26, Issue 1, pp. 829-841.

Walters, P. G. P. 1983, Export Information Sources – A Study of Their Usage and Utility, *International Marketing Review*, Issue Winter, pp. 34-43.

Watson, K. & Hogarth-Scott, S. 2003, *Understanding the Influence of Constraints to International Entrepreneurship in Small and Medium-Sized Export Companies, Frontiers of Entrepreneurship Research*, Research Working Papers.

Weaver, K. M. & Pak, J. 1990, Export Behavior and Attitudes of Small and Medium-Sized Korean Manufacturing Firms, *International Small Business Journal*, Vol. 8, Issue 4, pp. 59-70.

Weaver, K. M., Berkowitz, D. & Davies, L. 1998, Increasing the Efficiency of National Export Promotion Programs: The Case of Norwegian Exporters, *Journal of Small Business Management*, Vol. 36, Issue 4, pp. 1-12.

Welch, L. & Wiedersheim-Paul, F. 1980), Initial Exports – A Marketing Failure?, *The Journal of Management Studies*, Vol. 17, Issue 3, pp. 333-344.

Wengel, J. & Rodriguez, E. 2006, SME Export Performance in Indonesia After the Crisis, *Small Business Economics*, Vol. 26, Issue 1, pp. 25-37.

Westhead, P. 1995, Exporting Non-exporting Small Firms in Great Britain, *International Journal of Entrepreneurial Behavioral and Research*, Vol. 1, Issue 2, pp. 6-36.

Westhead, P., Binks, M. Ucbasaran, D., and Wright, M. 2002, Internationalisation of SMEs: A Research Note, *Journal of Small Business Enterprise Development*, Vol. 9, Issue 1, pp. 38-48.

Wie, T. K. 2000, The Impact of the Economic Crisis on Indonesia's Manufacturing Sector, *The Developing Economies*, Vol. 38, Issue 4, pp. 420-453.

Wie, T. K. 2006, Policies for Private Sectors Developments in Indonesia, ADB *Institute Discussion Paper* No. 46.

Wiedersheim-Paul, F., Olson, H. & Welch, L. S. 1978, Pre-export Activity: The First Step in Internationalisation, *Journal of International Business Studies*, Issue Spring/Summer, pp. 47-58.

Wignaraja, G. 2003, *Competitiveness Strategy in Developing Countries: A Manual for Policy Analysis*, Routledge, London.

Wignaraja, P. A. et al. 1991, *Participatory Development*, Oxford University Press, Karachi.

Wijaya, T. 2008, Kajian Model Empiris Perilaku Berwirausaha UKM DIY dan Jawa Tengah, *Journal of Management and Entrepreneurship*, Vol. 10, Issue 2, pp. 93-104.

Wilkinson, T. & Brouthers, L. E. 2006, Trade Promotion and SME Export Performance, *International Business Review*, Vol. 15, Issue 1, pp. 233-252.

Williams, D. A. 2008, Export Stimulation of Micro and Small Locally Owned Firms from Emerging Environments: New Evidence, *Journal of International Entrepreneurship*, Vol. 6, Issue 3, pp. 101-122.

Wolff, J. & Pett, T. L. 2000, Internationalisation of Small Firms: An Examination of Export-Strategy Approach, Firm Size, and Export Performance, *Journal of Small Business Management*, Vol. 38, Issue 2, pp. 34-47.

World Bank 1998, *Oil Windfalls: Blessing or Curse?* Oxford University Press, New York.

World Bank 1993, The *East Asian Miracle: Economic Growth and Public Policy*, Oxford University Press, New York.

World Bank 1991, *World Development Report*, Oxford University Press, New York.

World Development Indicator, viewed 4 January 2018, < http://0-ddp-ext.worldbank.org.library.newcastle.edu.au/ext/DDPQQ/report.do?method=showReport>.

WTO, World Trade Organisation statististics[1], viewed February 2016, <http://www.wto.org/english/news_e/pres10_e/pr598_e.htm>.

Wood, A. & Jordan, K. 2000, Why Does Zimbabwe Export Manufactures and Uganda Not? Econometrics Meets History, *The Journal of Development Studies*, Vol. 37, Issue 2, pp. 91-116.

World Trade Organisation, *Participation of developing countries in World Trade: Overview of major trends and underlying factors*, viewed June 2009, <http://www.wto.org/english/tratop_e/devel_e/w15.htm>.

Wortzel, L. H. & Wortzel, H. V. 1981, Export Marketing Strategies for NIC and LDC based Firms, *Columbia Journal of World Business*, Vol. pp. 51-59.

Yang, Y. S., Leone, R. P. & Alden, D. L. 1992, A Market Expansion Ability Approach to Identify Potential Exporters, Journal of Marketing, Vol. 56, Issue January, pp. 84-96.

Yaprak, A. 1985, An Empirical Study of the Differences Between Small Exporting and Non-Exporting US Firms, *International Marketing Review*, Vol. 2, Issue Summer, pp. 72-83.

Yeoh, P. L. 1994, Entrepreneurship and Export Performance: A Proposed Conceptual Model, in Axinn, C.N., editor, *Advances in International Marketing*, Vol. 6, JAI Press, Greenwich, CT, pp. 43-68.

Young, S. 1995, Export Marketing: Conceptual and Empirical Developments, *European Journal of Marketing*, Vol. 29, Issue 8, pp. 7-16.

Zhao, H. & Zou, S. 2002, The Impact of Industry Concentration and Firm Location on Export Propensity and Intensity: An Empirical Analysis of Chinese Manufacturing Firms, *Journal of International Marketing*, Vol. 10, Issue 1, pp. 52-71.

Zou, S. & Stan, S. 1998, The Determinants of Export Performance: A Review of the Empirical Literature between 1987 and 1997, *International Marketing Review*, Vol. 15, Issue 15, pp. 333-356.

Appendix 1: Managerial and Organisational Determinants of Export Propensity

	r	Unstandardized Coefficients		Standardized Coefficients	t	Sig.
		B	S.E.	βeta		
Export prop ‹— Amount of assets	0.263	0.282	0.143	0.126	1.972	**
Export prop ‹— Number of workers	0.171	0.000	0.000	-0.057	-0.965	NS
Export prop ‹— Geographic market devt	0.133	-0.180	0.052	-0.019	-0.342	NS
Export prop ‹— Firm age	0.125	0.008	0.01	0.051	0.856	NS
Export prop ‹— Location	-0.193	-0.315	0.142	-0.126	-2.226	**
Export prop ‹— Director's age	-0.016	-0.141	0.078	-0.106	-1.806	*
Export prop ‹— Director's education	0.208	0.128	0.128	0.065	0.995	NS
Export prop ‹— Director's experience abroad	0.092	-0.137	0.206	-0.040	-0.662	NS
Export prop ‹— Director's language prof.	0.238	-0.051	0.079	-0.044	-0.646	NS

Appendix 2: Managerial and Organisational Determinants of Export Intensity

		Unstandardized Coefficients		Standardized Coefficients		
	R	B	S.E.	Beta	T	Sig.
Export inty ‹— Amount of assets	0.426	0.111	0.063	0.068	1.743	*
Export inty ‹— Number of workers	0.241	0.000	0.000	-0.049	-1.355	NS
Export inty ‹— Geographic market devt	0.166	-0.001	0.023	-0.002	-0.058	NS
Export inty ‹— Firm age	0.062	-0.007	0.004	-0.062	-1.718	*
Export inty ‹— Location	-0.005	0.005	0.063	0.003	0.083	NS
Export inty ‹— Director's age	0.124	0.037	0.035	0.038	1.059	NS
Export inty ‹— Director's education	0.199	-0.013	0.057	-0.010	-0.236	NS
Export inty ‹— Director's experience abroad	0.182	-0.150	0.092	-0.061	-1.641	NS
Export inty ‹— Director's language proficiency	0.394	0.071	0.035	0.086	2.034	**

Made in the USA
Monee, IL
07 March 2026

45684909R00118